John Edward Bunch II
Black Dragon
Lifer
Retired National President
Former National Enforcer
Former East Coast Regional President
Original 7/President Atlanta Chapter
Mighty Black Sabbath MC Nation
A Breed Apart
Since 1974 and Still Strong………..///
www.bikerliberty.com
Host Black Dragon Biker TV YouTube
Host Black Dragon Biker Facebook
Host BlackDragonBikerTV Instagram
Host BlackDragonBikerTV TikTok
X.COM @jbunchii
Host The Dragon's Lair Motorcycle Chaos Podcast – Spreaker.com
Sales/Advertising 404.692.0336
blackdragon@blacksabbathmc.com
Bunch Media Group
P.O. 931792
Norcross, Ga 30003

24,453 words.

Motorcycle Club
Chaplain's Handbook
"The Cappellani"

- Edited: Christin Chapman
- Cover design:

First Edition, First Printing March 2026

Motorcycle Club Chaplain's Handbook

The Cappellani

By, John Edward Bunch II 'Black Dragon' BSFFBS

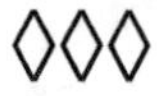

Motorcycle Club Chaplain's Handbook "The Cappellani" is the eleventh book in the Motorcycle Club Bible series. This manual teaches MC chaplaincy principles as the first professional guide to spiritual leadership inside the motorcycle club world. From confidentiality and crisis response to memorial ceremonies, mentorship, motorcycle club protocol, and inter-club diplomacy, this field manual gives MC Chaplains and officers practical tools to keep both soul and structure strong within the mighty MC Nation.

Bunch Media Group
Motorcycle Club Education Division

Library of Congress Control Number: **2026906843**
International Standard Book Number: **979-8-9991208-7-8**

◊◊◊

For information about special discounts for bulk purchases or club purchases please contact Bunch Media Group at

404.692.0336 or blackdragon@blacksabbathmc.com.

Black Dragon can speak at your live events, host your annual, teach at your MC protocol training sessions, or host your live events. For more information or to book an event contact Bunch Media Group at 404.692.0336 or
blackdragon@blacksabbathmc.com.
BlackDragonBikerTV - Instagram
Black Dragon Biker TV - YouTube
Black Dragon Biker - Facebook
BlackDragonBikerTV - TikTok
The Dragon's Lair Motorcycle Chaos Podcast
www.blackdragonsgear.com
www.bikerliberty.com

◊◊◊

This book was researched and written with the assistance of the Artificial Intelligence platform ChatGPT 5.1.

About the cover:
The cover was designed in ChatGPT by Gianfranco 'Moto-Gato' Medina of the Shot Gun LEMC Dallas, Texas. He has been a long time contributor to the Black Dragon Biker TV podcast. It depicts an MC Capellanus with his holy book in hand, staring at the sun rising or descending on the horizon behind a mountain. On his back are wings. In front of him is his motorcycle. He stands on strength, faith, and brotherhood. His faith brings calm to his brothers.

Acknowledgements:

Above all, I thank God. To Him be the glory.

- To my wife and my rock Tahmehrah 'Tia' 'Redbone' Bunch.
- To my editor Christin Chapman, 11 books strong!
- To my beloved mother Anese Yvonne Bunch.
- To the Father of the Black Sabbath Motorcycle Club Nation Paul 'Pep' Perry.
- To my beloved Aunt Bernita and Uncle JP Hall.
- To my daughter and grandson.
- To my former manager Jim Morgan. Jim hired me as a Technical Writer at ARRIS in 2005 where I worked for 16 years. When he saw I was writing a huge book called the Motorcycle Club's Bible he told me to instead write several smaller books calling them a series of MC bibles like ARRIS did with software, MSUPs and revisions. With that small bit of advice, reminding me of how things were done in corporate America, he enlightened me to launch a media empire far greater than one book, which has fed my family ever since. Thank you Jim.
- To Pastor Dr. Darrel 'Logic' Turner Founder/President of God's Warriors Motorcycle Ministry and Detroit Police Commissioner District 2 The Honorable Lavish T. Williams National Vice President of Boogie Down MC. Thank you both for your work as co-hosts on Black Dragon Biker TV.
- To Pastor Steve "Preacherman" Hill. Thank you for your assistance on this book.
- To my former shipmate USS Memphis SSN 691 Rev. C.J. Phillips. Thank you for your oversite on this book.
- To Rev. Barefoot preacher founder of Repented Motorcycle Ministry. Thank you for your oversite on this book.
- To Rev. Phil Redeemed Motorcycle Ministry. Thank you for your oversite on this book.

🏍 Who Should Read this Book?

1 – Motorcycle Club Chaplains and Those Preparing To Serve

This is the first and only definitive field guide for men and women called to be the moral and spiritual backbone of their clubs — whether traditional MCs, 1%er MCs, veterans' groups, or support clubs. It gives practical procedures, ceremonies, crisis responses, and the mindset of service beyond self.

2 – Club Presidents and Leadership Councils

Chapter officers will learn how to integrate an MC Chaplain into the command structure and use this position to maintain morale, unity, and discipline without compromising the chain of command.

3 – Prospects and New Members

Early reading reveals the deeper philosophy of MC life — loyalty, respect, and accountability — and prepares prospects for the brotherhood they're earning.

4 – Veteran and Service-Based Riding Organizations

Those coming from military or first-responder backgrounds will recognize familiar structure and conduct. This book adapts Professional Naval Chaplaincy concepts for the road.

5 – Members of Motorcycle Ministries

Christian and inter-faith motorcycle ministries often ride beside or interact with mainstream and outlaw MCs. This handbook equips ministry riders to understand MC protocol, speak the language of respect, and serve effectively without disrespecting boundaries.

6 – Independent Riders and Support Clubs

Even riders without formal club membership can use this handbook to understand MC culture, learn proper protocol, and apply the ethics of respect and discipline to their own riding groups.

7 – Law Enforcement, Community Leaders, and Researchers

For those studying or working alongside the MC community, this book reveals the order, honor, and purpose operating beneath the leather — knowledge essential to effective cooperation and mutual respect.

8 – Any Leader in High-Stress Brotherhoods

Firefighters, veterans, first responders, and clergy in tight-knit organizations will recognize shared truths about morale, balance, and servant leadership.

9 – Anyone Seeking Practical Leadership Grounded in Honor

Because the text combines MC experience, military chaplaincy ethics, and leadership science, it also works as a guide for any high-stress profession where loyalty, confidentiality, and composure are survival skills.

"If you ride with honor, lead with humility, or stand between chaos and calm — this book is for you."
— Black Dragon

Former National President
Black Sabbath Motorcycle Club Nation

◊◊◊

Author's Autograph

If you meet me in person I will gladly autograph this book for you! Thank you for purchasing it.

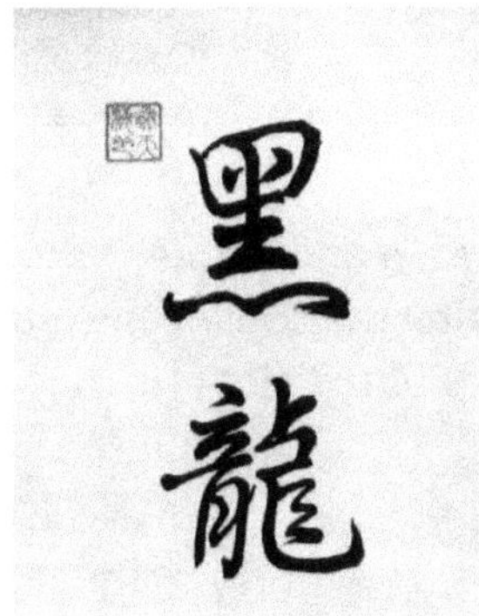

JBII

Dedication

One day I was on top of a mountain riding my motorcycle through the Tail of the Dragon with my blood brother John Pierre Bunch. Some men of God from Disciple Christian MM recognized me and asked if they could pray over my social media outreach. I have felt enriched and blessed in my communications ever since. The experience caused me to eventually write this book for the capellani.

Figure 1 Photo Courtesy Jon Pierre Bunch

This book was written for the men and women who dedicate themselves to nurturing the soul of the motorcycle club. The *cappellani!* Guardians of the cloak!

◊◊◊

Oversight

To the ordained Men of God, I asked to look over this work and provide me with oversight, advice, and counsel – I would like to say, "Thank you!" Your words, insight, criticism, and encouragement helped me to move forward confidently with this project.

God's Warriors Motorcycle Ministry Founder/President, Pastor, Reverand Dr. Darrel 'Logic' Turner, Emergency Response Chaplain Dallas, Texas

Former Silent Service shipmate **USS Memphis SSN 691** Hunter/Killer Fast Attack Submarine Los Angeles Class 688, Pastor Reverand C.J. Phillips of Washington D.C.

Repented Motorcycle Ministry Founder Reverand 'Barefoot Preacher.'

Repented Motorcycle Ministry National Chaplain, Reverand Phill 'P-Nut' Duttry Master of Theological Studies (MTS).

When a young chaplain met a grizzled 1%er he was given the following advice he shared with me:

"If you're gonna be a thug be a thug; if you're gonna be a Christian be a Christian. You can't be both."

◊◊◊

🏍 Foreword

"Some men preach about courage. Others ride into it."

For more than a century, the motorcycle community has carried a reputation that's larger than life — freedom lovers, fighters, veterans, outlaws, dreamers, and loyal friends bound by the miles between them.

In every generation, those miles have also carried loss, conflict, triumph, and redemption. And between the roar of engines and the silence of memory, there has always been one quiet figure keeping the brotherhood steady: the Chaplain.

Until now, he had no manual that truly spoke his language.
The Motorcycle Club Chaplain's Handbook closes that gap.
It's built from the same steel and integrity as the culture it serves — forged by a man who's walked both decks and clubhouses, worn both dolphins and patches, served his MC at the highest level, and understands discipline as a way of life.

John E. "Black Dragon" Bunch II doesn't write from imagination; he writes from scars and service.

He brings the structure of professional naval chaplaincy into the freedom of motorcycle clubs, proving that faith and respect can coexist even in the rawest subculture on the road.

This book is more than training; it's transformation.
It teaches Chaplains — and every club officer — how to anchor their brotherhood in principles that outlast trends and politics.
It speaks to all who lead in high-stress families: that loyalty, discipline, and compassion are not contradictions; they are the same road seen from different lanes.

You'll find here practical guidance on everything from accident scenes to memorial runs, from counseling to crisis diplomacy. But deeper than that, you'll find a call — the same call answered by every soldier, sailor, and biker who ever swore an oath: Serve somebody bigger than yourself.

Whether you wear a cross, a crescent, a star, or just a patch soaked in rain and miles, this handbook gives you the framework to lead with confidence, to stand with humility, and to bring peace without weakness into one of the toughest brotherhoods in the world. If you are reading this because you've been asked to become a Chaplain, congratulations — you've earned your club's trust. If you are reading it because you care about understanding the spirit that keeps riders bonded, you're in the right place. Either way, open these pages with respect, and you'll discover what true spiritual leadership looks like on two wheels.

Because in every clubhouse, every rally, and every open stretch of asphalt where brothers gather, someone must stand ready to guard the spirit of the patch. This handbook shows you how.

Black Dragon
— A fellow rider and brother of the wind

◊◊◊

Table of Contents

🏍 CHAPTER ONE
The Call to Serve

"Some men join a club to find a brotherhood. Some are called to guard it."

The Meaning of the Call

Every MC is more than engines, patches, and miles. It's a living organism—heart, soul, steel, and sweat bound together by loyalty. When a club grows, it needs people who can keep that heart beating steady. The Sergeant-at-Arms guards discipline, the President guides policy, the Road Captain conducts the pack, but the Chaplain guards the spirit.

No one volunteers for this calling just to look "righteous." The true call comes quietly. You notice the silence after a brother's funeral and realize someone has to say words that make sense of it. You see tempers swelling across a meeting table and feel the pull to calm the room before the first punch flies. You stand at a crash site and understand that courage and comfort ride in the same saddle. That's the moment the uniformed chaplain and the patched chaplain are born of the same purpose.

For me, that understanding started beneath the waves of the seven seas while patrolling the ocean's bottom aboard hunter/killer Los Angeles class nuclear attack submarines. Ten years in the Silent Service teaches you discipline, precision, and trust—three lifelines that carry straight into club life. A submarine runs on faith: faith in the boat, the crew, and the shipmate beside you and yes, for many, a faith in God. An MC runs the same way. When everything around you vibrates at the edge of control, faith—of any kind—keeps you balanced.

A Mission Without a Pulpit

Club chaplaincy isn't about sermons or theology; it's about presence. In the Navy we called it "deck-plate ministry." In a club, it's *shop-floor ministry*: wrench in one hand, open ear in the other. A chaplain doesn't parade scripture—he carries quiet authority earned from miles shared and promises kept.

Your mission is simple to say and hard to live:

- **Be there.** When brothers hurt, celebrate, or just need to talk at 2 a.m.
- **Keep counsel.** What's told in confidence stays locked up tight.
- **Speak truth.** Even when it costs popularity.
- **Uplift morale.** Remind the Club who it is when tempers or tragedy try to rewrite the story.

Duty and Discipline

Like every billet in a paramilitary family, chaplaincy demands discipline. You prepare for spiritual warfare the same way a seaman drills for fire or flood. Read, train, rehearse. Carry your Field Kit as faithfully as any mechanic carries tools. Know the difference between drama and danger, between gossip and a genuine cry for help.

The Chaplain never outranks anyone, but influence isn't about rank—it's about reliability. When a chaplain speaks, the Club should hear calm even when there's chaos. That steadiness earns authority one crisis at a time.

Serving the Entire Patch

The call doesn't filter by colors. The same code applies whether you wear a diamond, a veterans patch, or run independent. The Chaplain's lane runs through every part of the MC world because humanity runs through every club. You don't ask who's "approved" before you help a grieving rider; you simply stand in the space that needs filling.

Faith Beyond Religion

A Motorcycle Club Chaplain respects all beliefs and even riders who claim none. Brotherhood itself is sacred ground. When the Club bows its heads, you guide them—not toward religion, but toward reflection. Each man or woman decides what name to give their higher power; you just remind them to look for it.

The Weight and the Reward

It's easy to wear the patch proudly when the engines rumble and the sun's out. You earn your real respect in the long nights—when you carry news that breaks hearts, when you ride in the rain behind a hearse, when you hold steady between anger and reconciliation. That's the road few volunteer to ride, but the one the Chaplain must.

The reward isn't applause. It's the quiet nod from a brother whose life you steadied. It's knowing the Club slept a little easier because you were there. That's the unseen paycheck of the Chaplain's trade.

Your First Orders

1. Learn the Club's history, its victories, and its wounds.
2. Build credibility through service, not talk.
3. Keep a strong back and a soft heart.
4. Train like someone's life may depend on your calm—because one day it might.
5. Remember that every time you put on your cut, you represent the spirit of every rider who ever took this oath.

"The road doesn't ask for perfection; it asks for presence. The call to serve is answered not by words, but by wheels that keep rolling when others stop."

◊◊◊

🏍 CHAPTER TWO

The Origin of the Chaplain: From the Cloak of Martin to the Colors of the Club

"Every title has a story.
The story behind 'Chaplain' begins with a cloak and a soldier."

A Soldier's Gesture

Back in the fourth century, a young Roman cavalry officer named Martin of Tours rode the boundary between power and poverty. One bitter winter day he saw a beggar shivering outside the city gate. Martin had no money, no food—just the heavy wool cloak issued to every soldier.
He drew his sword, cut the cloak in two, and wrapped one half around the man. That night, legend says, Martin dreamed of Christ wearing the torn half of that cloak and saying to the angels, *"See how Martin has clothed me."*
That act became a symbol—**compassion expressed through courage**.

The Cloak and the Word

After Martin left the army and devoted his life to ministry, the half-cloak he had shared became a relic, carried into battle by the kings of the Franks to remind them that mercy must ride alongside might. The Latin word for cloak—*cappa*—gave name to the small temporary tents where it was kept. Those small tents or small churches came to be known as chapels: the *capella.*

The clerics who tended that relic and prayed for the soldiers were called *cappellani* — the guardians of the cloak.
Over time, *cappellanus* in Latin evolved into the French *chapelain*, and finally into the English chaplain.
So in the beginning, the chaplain wasn't a priest behind stone walls. He was a **field companion who guarded a fragment of compassion among warriors**.

From Battlefield to Brotherhood

Centuries later, the title traveled with armies, navies, and fleets. Chaplains stood in the mud of Agincourt, on the decks of wooden ships, and in the trenches of Europe—not preaching doctrine, but carrying presence, hope, and human decency into chaos.
When the modern armed services formed formal Chaplain Corps—like the Navy Chaplain Corps whose guides shape this handbook—the same principle survived: **care for the morale, spirit, and dignity of the unit**.

The Parallels with Motorcycle Club Culture

Every motorcycle club, especially those with paramilitary roots, mirrors that structure of comradeship in arms.

- The **colors** resemble banners.
- The **patch** hierarchy mirrors a chain of command.
- The **rides and runs** are long deployments shared under risk, weather, and watchfulness.
- The wars some clubs engage mirror the campaigns fought by militaries.

Within that structure, the MC Chaplain inherits precisely the same mantle as Martin's *cappellani:* protector of compassion inside a brotherhood of warriors.

Where the ancient chaplains carried a fragment of a cloak, today's MC Chaplain may carry a patch, a coin, or a piece of cloth from a fallen brother's cut—each a reminder that mercy and loyalty must never be strangers.

What the Etymology Teaches

The language itself carries the mission:

- **Chapel (capella)** once meant *field tent*.
- **Chaplain (cappellanus)** originally meant *caretaker of the camp's soul.*
- The **cloak—*cappa***—symbolized shelter and warmth, offered even at personal cost.

So, when an MC Chaplain steps forward, he joins a line that began with **a soldier who cut his comfort in half**. The uniform may change—chain mail, dress blues, leather vest—but the job description hasn't: *to guard the spirit of those who ride into risk.*

Modern Echoes

That single story, told for seventeen centuries, gives context to why the title commands respect regardless of religion. Whether you follow Christian faith, another path, or none, every Chaplain stands for the same timeless principle: serve those who serve others. When an MC Chaplain blesses a ride, comforts a widow, or listens to a brother wrestling with demons, he continues the work that began with Martin's blade and broken cloak—**turning strength into service.**

Reflection

"They called the first chaplains guardians of a cloak. We carry that same duty wrapped in leather and road dust. Different uniform, same promise:
Never forget the man standing in the cold."

◊◊◊

🏍 CHAPTER THREE
The Chaplain's Personal Habits and Conduct

"Long before anyone hears your words, they watch your walk."

The Standard You Carry

A Chaplain's authority doesn't come from a title or a cross; it comes from trust.
That trust is earned through habits—the daily disciplines that make a leader consistent, calm, and credible.

The Navy Chaplain's Manual teaches that the chaplain must be *above reproach in conduct, sound in judgment, and balanced in life.* For the Motorcycle Club Chaplain, that still applies—only the uniform is different.
Your life is your pulpit; your character, the sermon.

1. Personal Discipline

Every Club member values discipline, but the Chaplain lives it outwardly.

- **Punctuality:** Show up early; it broadcasts respect.
- **Cleanliness and appearance:** You don't need to look polished—you need to look intentional. Even in leather, keep your patch, gear, and self squared away. You should smell approachable. What brother wants to whisper his secrets when your breath is so offensive he must turn his head to catch a breath? If you reek of alcohol you cannot expect to be invited into a brother's personal space.

- Sobriety and restraint: Enjoy the celebration but keep your clarity. When everyone else loosens up, you stay steady.
- Language: Keep it real but measured. The right word delivered calmly carries more authority than any vulgarity laden string of insults.

Discipline isn't for image—it keeps you ready. The brothers trust a Chaplain who's always switched on, even at midnight on the side of the road.

2. Integrity and Accountability

Frazier wrote that the military chaplain must be "an example in personal honesty; one who neither exaggerates nor conceals."

In the MC world, honesty is currency. You can lose respect in one sentence if your words are unreliable.

- Tell the truth even when inconvenient.
- If you make a mistake, own it first.
- If you promise privacy, guard it even under pressure.

Your reputation becomes the measure of your ministry.

3. Confidential Trust

Nothing will define—or destroy—you faster than how you handle private words.

The Navy Chaplain's Code lists "confidential communication" as sacred law.
The MC Chaplain inherits that fully. Members must know they can talk to you without risk of gossip or retaliation.

- **Never repeat, never hint, never imply.**
- **Share only with explicit permission or in cases of danger to life.**
- When in doubt, seek counsel discreetly from senior leadership without revealing identities.

Without confidentiality, there is no chaplaincy—only rumor.

4. Balanced Loyalty

A Navy chaplain serves both God and Command; an MC Chaplain serves both Conscience and Club.
Balancing those loyalties is the hardest part of the job.

Sometimes leadership asks for advice that conflicts with what's right. Sometimes a brother wants help that endangers the Club. Your loyalty must be twofold:

- **To the Club's welfare first**, not its temporary politics.
- **To universal moral truth**, not one man's convenience.

A Chaplain without moral balance becomes a politician. Keep your footing.

5. Temperament and Self-Control

Frazier emphasized calm disposition: a Chaplain must be *"not easily excited, quick to sympathize, slow to condemn."*
That's your daily drill.

The Club feeds off your tone.
In chaos, you breathe deep.
In conflict, you lower your voice when others raise theirs.
True control isn't about ruling others—it's about mastering self.

6. Professional Growth

Military chaplains drill, study, and train constantly. So should you. Read across belief systems, leadership manuals, history, and psychology.
Ride with different chapters, meet other Chaplains, vets, or clergy. Every person teaches something about compassion or competence.

Growth earns respect. Ignorance breeds irrelevance.

7. Family and Personal Life

You cannot hold others together if your own foundation crumbles. Protect your home relationships. Keep communication honest. Guard rest, health, and prayer—or whatever your form of reflection.
When your personal life is balanced, your counsel carries clarity rather than projection.

8. Financial and Social Conduct

Handle money carefully, favors sparingly. Never blend spiritual and financial gain.
Within the Club, avoid borrowing, lending, or gambling that could challenge neutrality.
Generosity is strength; manipulation is poison.

Be social, but never *sloppy*. The Chaplain who crosses emotional or romantic lines within the Club loses authority permanently.

Remember this: *You represent restraint in a world built on motion.*

9. Presence on the Road

Ride how you live: predictable, disciplined, and loyal. A chaplain stunting in the pack, engaging in reckless endangerment, and unnecessarily risking lives does not demonstrate compassion for life or the safety of brothers on the road and is unsuitable to carry the title.

- Maintain gear and situational awareness.
- Assist in breakdowns and first-aid readiness.
- Lead by example at stops, ceremonies, and community events.

Your handling of the road tells everyone how you handle life.

10. Spiritual Readiness

Whatever your faith expression, keep it sharp.
Pray, meditate, reflect, ride alone sometimes. A Chaplain whose own tank is empty can't refuel anyone else.
The Navy Chaplain's Manual said, *"Before one can minister to others, he must guard the fire of his own spirit."*
That's still true on the back of a Harley.

Summary Principle

Be the same man in daylight and darkness.
Conduct that is steady builds trust that is unbreakable.
The MC Chaplain should embody calm action, clean conscience, quick humor, and quiet faith.

The stronger your habits, the more naturally respect follows—because everyone can fake charisma, but nobody can fake consistency.

Reflection

"A Chaplain's greatest sermon is how he lives. Whether in a submarine or on a highway, the crew measures him by conduct long before creed."

◊◊◊

🏍 Bridge Reflection — From Habits to Brotherhood

"The habits of the Chaplain shape the heartbeat of the Club. Before you tune the Club's soul, make sure your own instrument rings true."

Before moving from your personal conduct to the Club's moral backbone, pause here. A chaplain who cannot lead himself will never hold a brotherhood together. Use this page as your pre-ride inspection for the soul — a way to check your own systems before guiding others.

⚙ **Dragon's Pre-Ride Tip**

"Every Club mirrors its Chaplain.
If you walk steady, brothers find their footing.
If your attitude wobbles, the whole line drifts.
Check your balance before you twist the throttle."*

Self-Inspection Checklist

(Quick-reference bullets for training logs or meeting devotionals.)

- **Mind :** Am I clear, rested, and sober?
- **Mouth :** Are my words lifting or dividing today?
- **Mood :** Am I carrying calm into the room?
- **Mission :** Do I remember that serving the Club means serving its soul?

Five minutes of self-check prevents miles of moral repair work.

1. Mirror Check — Personal Discipline

Ask yourself:

- Do my daily routines show the steadiness I preach?
- Have I kept my language, appearance, and attitude consistent with the respect I expect from others?
- Would I trust advice coming from a man who behaves like me on his worst day?

Goal: Catch any cracks in your own armor before someone else does.

2. Fuel Gauge — Spiritual Energy

- Have I refueled my own spirit lately, or am I trying to run on fumes?
- What habits restore my patience — prayer, solitude, the open road, music, study?
- When I get tired or cynical, who or what do I lean on for balance?

Goal: A depleted chaplain transmits burnout; a centered one transmits strength.

3. Maintenance Log — Relationships

- Have I repaired small misunderstandings before they became grudge matches?
- Am I fair in listening to leadership and to rank-and-file equally?

- Do members still approach me freely, or am I becoming distant or judgmental?

Goal: Keep the lines open; corrosion of trust starts quietly.

4. Road Conditions — Club Atmosphere

- Is morale rising or dipping around me?
- Do I sense bitterness, pride, or fatigue infecting the group?
- What quiet influence can I apply right now to steady the temperature?

Goal: Recognize moral weather changes before the storm hits.

5. Chain Tension — Balance of Compassion and Discipline

- Am I too soft on disorder or too harsh with weakness?
- Have I corrected with love as much as I've comforted with strength?

Goal: Keep the chain just tight enough to transmit power without snapping.

Action Note

If you find slippage in any category, adjust immediately. Revisit your Personal Habits and Conduct goals, reset, then move forward. The Club will mirror what you model—never forget that every calm decision, every consistent moment of respect, becomes part of the moral backbone you're about to defend.

"The next chapter belongs to the Club.
Make sure the man entering it is ready."

◊◊◊

🏍 CHAPTER FOUR
The Moral Backbone of the Club: Spirit, Discipline, and Code

"When the road tests the brotherhood, it's the backbone that keeps the body upright. The habits of one man can steady the hearts of many."

After shaping your own conduct, the next mission is to guard the conduct of the brotherhood itself. The Chaplain's personal standard becomes the foundation for the Club's moral backbone—the network of unseen values that keeps a patch family standing when everything else shakes.

The Living Code

Every Club, no matter its patch, has two sets of rules: those written on paper and those written in blood, sweat, and memories.
The written ones keep order; the unwritten ones keep *meaning*.
The Chaplain's calling is to understand both, live both, and repair either one when time or pride starts to wear them thin.
A strong moral backbone means:

- Members act right even when unobserved.
- Leadership earns respect instead of demanding it.
- Conflict can rage without destroying unity.

When that backbone slips disrespect, distrust, and disunity follow fast. It's your watch to see those fractures forming before anyone else does.

Spirit — The Power Source

In the military they talk about "unit morale."
In club life, we call it *spirit* — the invisible spark that keeps brothers showing up, wrenching late, riding long, and defending each other on bad days.
You can't measure spirit in miles or money.
You recognize it by the look in a man's eyes when somebody says, "We ride at dawn," and he quietly nods *yes*.

As Chaplain, you feed that spirit:

- Start your day with gratitude, end it with respect.
- Catch good behavior in action and praise it.
- Speak peace into tense rooms before voices rise.
- Remind the Club why it rides, not just where.

When you protect spirit, you protect identity.

Discipline — The Frame That Carries Freedom

Spirit gives motion; *discipline* keeps the machine from flying apart. Freedom without discipline is just noise. Discipline turns freedom into purpose.

A disciplined Club:

- Honors hierarchy and chain of command.
- Respects property, time, and protocols.
- Handles internal correction quietly and fairly.

A Chaplain models discipline by calm consistency.
Turn up on time. Keep your patch clean. Ride within formation.
People watch you more closely than anyone else — if your lines are straight, others will straighten theirs.

Remember: discipline isn't domination.
It's a promise to each other that chaos will never drive the Club.

Code — The Law of the Road

Call it code, creed, or protocol – whatever name it carries, it boils down to this:
Loyalty, Respect, Honor, and Duty.
It's not religion, but it is sacred.
It lives in how brothers treat each other, how they ride in traffic, and how they speak when another Club's patch enters the room.
The Chaplain becomes the living conscience of that code.
When tempers flare or greed whispers, your calm reminder of principle can turn a near-disaster into just another story told long after the run.

Reading the Moral Weather

The best Chaplains develop radar: they sense a shift before the storm breaks.

Watch for:

- Sharp sarcasm replacing humor.
- Members skipping meetings without reason.
- Clusters forming that exclude others.
- Leadership burnout or detachment.

When you feel those tremors, act quietly. A simple *"How you doing, brother?"* in the parking lot can stop a quake before it starts.

Handling Breaches of the Code

You're not the lawman — you're the conscience.
Your approach should be private, respectful, and direct.

1. Observe. Get facts, not gossip.
2. Guide. Ask questions that lead men to see consequences.
3. Support leadership. Report only when integrity or safety demands it.
4. Restore. Once correction happens, help heal the wound so no grudges linger.

Discipline restores order; forgiveness restores unity.
Without both, nothing holds together.

The Chaplain's Influence on Culture

Culture is caught, not taught. A thousand quiet examples outweigh one speech.

You change a clubhouse by how you live inside it:

- Keep humor clean but sharp.
- Show respect to every prospect; it teaches officers humility.
- Ride every mile you can. Presence earns credibility.
- Demonstrate that faith and freedom can share the same throttle.

When tradition drifts from value, you steer it back without tearing it down. That's true leadership.

Dragon's Field Note

"The Club's backbone isn't built in ceremonies; it's built in repetition.
Every time a man keeps his word, discipline tightens.
Every time a brother forgives, spirit strengthens.
Every time a Chaplain stays calm, code survives."

Exercise — Backbone Check

Purpose: to give Chaplains and officers a quick readiness picture of the Club's moral health.

Rate each item 0-5 (0 = nonexistent 5 = strong):

Category	**0–5**	**Notes**
Member respect across ranks		
Meeting discipline (starts / ends on time, protocol respected)		
Spirit at runs (enthusiasm, inclusion, laughter)		
Conflict resolution (no lingering grudges)		
Community reputation (respected or avoided?)		
Chaplain accessibility (members approach freely)		

Tally results quarterly. Anything averaging under 3 needs attention. Review with leadership and develop action steps — no blame, just maintenance.

Reflection

"Spirit keeps us alive.
Discipline keeps us together.
The Code gives our miles meaning.
Break one, and the patch is just fabric;
keep them all, and the Club becomes legend."

End-of-Chapter Summary:

- The Chaplain's habits (Ch. 3) power Chapter 4's mission.
- Monitor morale, reinforce discipline, protect the Code.
- Lead with consistency; correct with compassion.
- A strong moral backbone outlasts any leadership change.

◊◊◊

🏍 CHAPTER FIVE
Command and Counsel: The Chaplain's Dual Allegiance

"A Chaplain walks two roads at once—one that reports upward, and one that reaches outward."

The Two Chains of Loyalty

In every organized brotherhood there are two chains:

1. **Command** — authority and decision.
2. **Counsel** — truth and conscience.

The Navy Chaplain answers both to Commanding Officer and to conscience.

The MC Chaplain mirrors that same structure.

- One loyalty belongs to the **President and governing council**, representing order.
- The other loyalty belongs to the **soul of the Club**, representing integrity.

Your challenge is walking between them without tearing either link.

Allegiance No. 1 — Serving Command

The Chaplain does not issue orders—but he upholds them.
You support leadership's mission by:

- Being a **confidential adviser**, not an echo chamber.
- Reinforcing decisions once they're made.
- Helping translate leadership intention into member understanding.
- Defending the President's authority in public, even when you question a choice in private.

Leadership trusts you because you tell the truth privately and represent unity publicly. That's how command cohesion survives opinion.

Allegiance No. 2 — Serving Conscience

Command keeps the Club functioning; conscience keeps it honorable. When policy clashes with principle, your duty is **clarity without rebellion**.

Ask yourself three questions before every moral decision:

1. *Is this action consistent with the Club's values and code?*
2. *Does it protect the long-term integrity of the patch?*
3. *Can I explain it to a widow, a child, or a judge without shame?*

If all three answers aren't clear *yes*, you know where to stand.

You may sometimes face impossible intersections—loyalty to a friend versus truth to leadership, or silence versus safety. When that happens, remember: **integrity with respect beats compliance with regret**.

The Art of Counsel

Counsel is not command; it's persuasion grounded in wisdom. The Chaplain becomes the **quiet strategist** who helps others see clearly what their emotions hide.

1. **Private Audience** – Request quiet moments, never challenge leaders in front of troops.
2. **Facts First** – Bring information and perspective, not gossip.
3. **Calm Tone** – Military calm works better than moral sermonizing.
4. **Offer Options** – Present paths, not ultimatums.
5. **Accept Outcome** – If command decides differently, respect the chain—even when you disagree.

"Your job is to advise with clarity and stand with loyalty."

Advising Leadership Under Pressure

When a Club faces heat—media, law-enforcement attention, public conflict—your counsel becomes crucial.

- Encourage leaders to pause before response.
- Remind them that respect lost in one rash press release may take years to rebuild.
- Help draft calm, factual statements or internal addresses.
- Stand visible beside leadership during hard times to show unity without arrogance.

Presence equals peace. When they see your calm posture, others lower their adrenaline.

Advising the Rank and File

Members often test new Chaplains: "Whose side are you on?" The correct answer is *The Club's side,* not any one faction's.

When advising members:

- Listen first; never promise outcomes you can't deliver.
- Encourage respect for proper channels.
- Translate leadership decisions into plain sense, minus politics.
- When someone needs correction, deliver it privately, not performatively.

Members learn that you are safe to talk to—but not safe to manipulate.

Conflict Between Chains

Eventually, command and counsel will collide.
It might be a disciplinary case, a leadership burn-out, or a moral gray zone.

Use this triage process:

Step 1 – **Clarify the Issue**.
Strip rumor and emotion from fact.

Step 2 – **Consult the Code**.
Revisit Club bylaws and moral backbone principles.

Step 3 – **Seek Quiet Dialogue First**.
Engage leadership privately before escalation.

Step 4 – **Protect Life and Honor First**.
If someone's safety or the Club's survival is at stake, act or speak decisively.

Step 5 – **Document Reflection**.
Record ethical reasoning in your Field Journal for training and accountability.
This sequence grounds you under stress; no panic decisions.

Ethical Neutrality

Maintaining neutrality doesn't mean hiding opinions; it means preventing favoritism.
You attend officer meetings as adviser, but you don't vote.
You mentor prospects, but you don't coach sides in political fights.
Your moral credibility survives only if everyone knows you'll treat them fair—even those you personally dislike.

Confidential Channels

The Chaplain can become bridge or barrier depending on speech discipline. **Develop three lanes of communication**:

Lane	Flow	Example
Vertical	President ↔ Chaplain	Leadership counsel, crisis updates
Horizontal	Members ↔ Chaplain	Personal or morale conversations
External	Community ↔ Chaplain	Public blessings, civic or veteran events

Never mix lanes; never let information cross without consent. That's operational security for both integrity and respect.

Respecting Authority and Autonomy

A Chaplain provides spiritual command presence without command rank. you lead by influence, not order. Honor the officers by letting them lead; strengthen them by helping them see. If you feel strongly about changing a policy, frame it as *mission enhancement*, not moral superiority. People resist preaching but respond to professionalism.

Maintaining Boundaries

Your post invites private access—use it wisely.

- Never become a messenger between arguing factions.
- Never allow counseling sessions to turn into gossip.
- Keep emotional distance when dealing with club families or supporters.
- Decline favors that blur neutrality.

Boundaries protect authenticity. When everyone knows the line, everyone feels safe crossing the Chaplain's doorstep.

Working with the Sgt-at-Arms and PRO

- Sergeant-at-Arms: coordinates discipline and security; you complement him by managing morale and emotional de-escalation.
  If he enforces, you restore.
- Public Relations Officer: handles public image; you handle spiritual image.
  If he defends the brand, you preserve the soul.

Shared information between you three prevents both fights and PR disasters.

Dragon's Leadership Note

"A Chaplain's voice is never the loudest in the room; it's the one people remember when noise fades."

Field Exercise — Dual Allegiance Drill

Purpose: train Chaplains to manage conflicting loyalties under stress.

Scenario: The President issues a disciplinary suspension that most members see as unfair.
Goal: Advise leadership while calming dissent.

Steps:

1. Meet privately with the President; present feedback without accusations.
2. Address the Club collectively—remind them discipline holds the line.
3. Provide separate space for grievances; let people speak safely.
4. After tensions cool, mediate a follow-up meeting for understanding, not reversal.

Record in Field Journal:
- What emotions surfaced?
- What words diffused tension?
- What would you modify next time?

This single exercise builds real-world resilience.

Reflection

"Command gives the Club direction; conscience gives it destination. The Chaplain rides between the two, steering steady when authority leans too hard or when conscience drifts too soft.
In that narrow lane lives the real ministry of brotherhood."

◊◊◊

🏍 CHAPTER SIX
Care and Counsel: The Chaplain as a Confidant and Crisis Responder

"Brotherhood isn't proven on perfect days; it's built in the middle of breakdowns, fights, funerals, and fear."

The Core Mission

Every Chaplain spends most of his time doing one of two things:

1. **Listening in peace.**
2. **Steadying in chaos.**

The first builds trust.
The second proves it.

When a Chaplain listens, he provides care.
When he steadies, he provides counsel.
When he does both well, the Club survives storms that would otherwise break it apart.

Confidant of the Brotherhood

The MC world runs on earned respect; nobody opens up to a stranger.
You won't become the Club's confidant because of your patch—it happens one quiet conversation at a time.

Principles of Confidential Care

1. **Availability.** Make yourself easy to reach but never invasive. Don't chase stories; invite honesty.
2. **Safe Presence.** Choose neutral ground—a smoke break, a garage corner, the tailgate after a ride. Set tone by sitting, not towering.
3. **Active Listening.** Hear words, but also watch hands, eyes, breath. A man's body tells what his pride hides.
4. **No Judgment.** Everyone in a Club has done something wild enough that only a brother should hear it. Reinstill dignity, not shame.
5. **Boundaries.** Know where spiritual counsel ends and professional help begins. When a member's issue passes beyond your training—addiction, mental health, domestic matters—help connect him discretely to proper aid.

"You're not a savior; you're a steady friend with resources."

Crisis Response in the MC Environment

Road life means real risk. Accidents, raids, sudden deaths, PTSD, incarceration—these are the Chaplain's battlefields.

1. At the Scene

- **Arrive steady.** Everyone watches your face first. If you panic, they panic.
- **Assess safety.** Before words, ensure hazards are controlled: fuel, traffic, tempers.

- **Touch carefully.** If medical help is active, stay clear of their work. Your ministry is emotional triage.
- **Words of calm.** Simple phrases—"We've got you." "Help's on the way." "Breathe, brother."—anchor reality.
- **Coordinate solidarity.** Keep spectators useful: block traffic, gather belongings, call families.
- **Pray or reflect if invited, never imposed.**

2. After the Crisis

- **Debrief quietly.** Assist officers with information and facts, not emotion.
- **Revisit witnesses privately.** Shock delayed will surface as anger or guilt; check in days later.
- **Follow up on long-term grief.** Anniversaries, birthdays of fallen brothers—be the one who remembers.

Presence outlives emergencies.

The Counseling Mindset

Military chaplains define counseling as *"a professional dialogue leading to understanding, healing, and action."*
Your version operates in garages, bars, parking lots, and ride sweeps — but the aim is the same: restore balance.

Types of Conversations

Category	**Example Situation**	**Chaplain's Approach**
Situational Stress	Loss of job, breakup, jail time	Listen, normalize reaction, plan forward steps
Moral Conflict	Brother betrays trust	Clarify feelings, outline options, reinforce code
Spiritual Drift	Loss of meaning or faith	Ask what used to inspire him, reconnect to purpose
Interpersonal Conflict	Officer/Member tension	Separate sides, mediate with fairness and respect
Trauma/PTSD	Flashbacks, insomnia, rage	Offer empathy, breathing control, refer if severe

Keep every talk short, clear, and constructive.
End with an achievable goal—*"Tonight you rest. Tomorrow we talk options."*

The Listening Technique

Your greatest weapon is silence.

1. **Listen**—uninterrupted for at least two minutes.
2. **Reflect**—"So what I hear you saying is ..."
3. **Clarify**—Ask neutral questions: *"What happened next?" "Who else has noticed?"*
4. **Confirm hope.** Always finish with reinforcement: *"We'll tackle this one mile at a time."*

Avoid clichés or quoting texts unless invited. Authenticity beats ritual.

Handling Self-Destructive Talk

If a brother says he's done riding for good, or talks about "ending it," never ignore it.

Immediate steps:

- Keep him with you; never isolate.
- Remove weapons, alcohol, keys if safely possible.
- Contact emergency services or mental-health crisis line; explain you're staying on site.
- Notify leadership afterward, not before.
- Follow up daily until professional help connects.

You don't break confidentiality—you preserve life.

Club Conflict Mediation

Disputes are inevitable. The Chaplain becomes *referee of reason.*

Method:

- Hear both sides separately first.
- Clarify points of agreement—always 1-2 exist.
- Reframe grievances as shared solutions: *"We both love this Club; we just see different roads."*
- Close with handshake or mutual statement of respect.

Document outcomes privately. No paperwork ever leaves your notebook without consent.

Preventive Care — Ministry of Presence

The best counseling happens before problems grow.

Ways to practice preventive presence:

- Ride in every event possible—visibility equals availability.
- Visit members during recoveries or confinement.
- Text check-ins: short, sincere, no preaching.
- Organize informal reflection nights: barbecue, fire pit, open talk.
- Coordinate with other Chaplains regionally for shared rides of healing.

This ongoing presence builds moral immunity within the Club.

Follow-Up and Documentation

Borrowed from military chaplain procedure:

- **Confidential Log:** Date, topic (category only), action, follow-up date. No names in written form.
- **Referral Record:** Keep list of trusted counselors, clergy, VA contacts, legal aid.
- **After-Action Review:** Post-incident reflection—what went well, what needs sharpening.

These habits preserve integrity and ensure uniform care as the Club grows.

Dragon's Field Observation

"A Chaplain doesn't fix people; he keeps them from breaking further until they remember their own strength."

Exercise — The Counseling Drill

Conduct monthly practice sessions with new Chaplains or officers.

1. Pair up; one plays the brother in crisis, one the Chaplain.
2. Use a prompt card (injury, marital stress, leadership conflict).
3. Role-play a 10-minute talk using active-listening cycle.
4. Switch roles.
5. Debrief: What tone built trust? What phrases triggered defense?

Record insights in Field Journal for mentorship reviews.

Reflection

"The Chaplain is the ear that listens when engines stop, the voice that steadies when courage trembles, and the hand that reminds every rider he's still part of the pack."

End-of-Chapter Summary

Care = Presence. Counsel = Process.

- Protect confidentiality; act decisively for safety.
- Maintain professional limits; refer when needed.
- Stay visible, calm, and sincere—the road always tests those three.
- Document quietly, mentor actively.

◊◊◊

🏍 CHAPTER SEVEN
Crisis and Combat Stress:
Supporting Brothers in Trauma and Loss

"No one rides forever, but no one rides alone in pain."

The Nature of the Battle

Every generation of men in uniform has learned that shared danger leaves invisible marks. The same is true for riders: accidents survived, funerals attended, violent run-ins, guilt when one brother falls and another walks away.

Those moments don't always leave scars you can see.
They leave noise that never shuts off inside the helmet.
That noise is combat stress, and in the MC world it wears no ribbons — just the look in a man's eyes when the laughter fades.

The Chaplain's mission is to recognize it early, guide brothers through it, and keep those ghosts from running the Club.

Understanding Stress and Trauma

Type	Description	MC Examples
Acute Stress	Sudden shock after an event; short-term disruption.	Bike wreck, fight, arrest, death notification.
Cumulative Stress	Built-up pressure from daily chaos.	Financial strain, long haul miles, home tension, leadership fatigue.
Moral Injury	Inner conflict when action or inaction violates one's own values.	loyalty vs. justice conflict, escalation gone wrong, survivor guilt.
Post-Traumatic Stress	Ongoing reaction beyond normal recovery.	Flashbacks, nightmares, avoidance, hyper-vigilance.

Your goal isn't diagnosis — it's recognition.
See it, name it quietly, respond early.

The Chaplain's Role in Crisis

1. **Stabilize the Immediate.**
   - Use calm tone, few words.
   - Secure physical safety first.
   - Breathe together — "In... out..." resets the body before the mind can follow.
2. **Contain the Emotion.**
   - Give permission to feel. Don't tell them to "man up."
   - Guide toward controlled release: deep breaths, walk, mechanical tasks.
3. **Restore Connection.**
   - Never leave a struggling brother isolated.
   - Bring in trusted members who can sit quiet without preaching.
4. **Monitor the Aftermath.**
   - Check in 24, 48, and 72 hours later.
   - Listen for guilt, numbness, or avoidance.
   - Encourage small routines: ride short, eat, sleep — physical rhythm rebuilds inner rhythm.

Recognizing the Warning Signals

When you hear:

- "I should've died instead."
- "It doesn't matter anymore."
- "I'm done riding."
  or when you see:
- Withdrawal from Club life.
- Heavy drinking alone.
- Reckless riding.
- Quick temper or blank stare —
  those are distress flares.

Respond, don't delay.
Step in respectfully but firmly: *"Brother, I can see something's chewing you up. Let's talk."*

The Long Road of Grief

For every crash, bust, or cancer fight, someone rides away with an empty saddle beside him. The Chaplain becomes the keeper of that space.

Stages of grief aren't a checklist — denial, anger, bargaining, depression, acceptance — they act more like gears: you shift back and forth between them without order.
Your job is to keep the gearbox from seizing.

Ways to help:

- **Presence:** visit, ride by, sit silent.
- **Commemoration:** host yearly candle ride or moment of revving silence.
- **Legacy building:** help the Club create scholarships, patches, or runs in the brother's name.
- **Permission:** remind them that joy isn't betrayal; laughter is part of healing.

"You honor the dead best by helping the living get moving again."

Working with PTSD and Chronic Trauma

You're not a clinician, but you can be a lifeline.

Approach:

1. Listen without analysis.
2. Validate that what they feel makes sense given what they lived.
3. Encourage professional help — position it as *"adding another wrench to the toolbox,"* not weakness.
4. Stay involved: check appointments, celebrate progress.

Build a contact roster:

- VA and Vet Centers.
- Trauma-trained therapists who respect biker culture.
- Peer-support riders' groups.
- Crisis hotlines and emergency numbers (national & local).

Keep it in your phone and in the Field Kit binder.

Funeral and Final Honors

When a member dies, the Chaplain leads the Club through three missions:

1. Honor the fallen.
2. Comfort the living.
3. Preserve the Club's dignity.
4. Be the bridge between the family and the Club helping the family to understand just how much their loved one was loved and respected.

Note: Sometimes a family hates the Club for "taking the brother away from them," or perhaps they feel the Club caused his death because if he wasn't in a motorcycle club he wouldn't have died on a motorcycle or in a scuffle involving the MC. In those cases, they may not even want the Club around in any way to celebrate the home going. These will be waters for the chaplain to navigate.

Coordinate with family first; respect their wishes.
Prepare service outline (see Blessing Templates chapter).
Encourage participation: each member doing one small act — carrying colors, reading a name, firing engines — helps transformation from helplessness to ceremony.

After the service, maintain connection. Grief returns quiet after crowds fade.

The Chaplain's Self-Care in Crisis

Repeated exposure to loss drains even seasoned Chaplains.
You must guard your own mental field.

Tactics:

- **After-action decompression:** private talk with another Chaplain or trusted veteran.
- **Physical grounding:** walk, ride solo, exercise.
- **Creative outlet:** write, wrench, play music.
- **Spiritual recharge:** whatever revives peace — prayer, meditation, long road.

If symptoms of burnout appear (insomnia, irritability, detachment), treat yourself as you'd treat a brother: acknowledge, rest, get help.

"You can't pour calm from an empty tank."

Dragon's Operational Note

"Trauma teaches ugly lessons. But within the pain there's a map — where loyalty, mortality, and love intersect. The Chaplain reads that map for others until they can see it again."

Exercise – The Critical-Incident Drill

Objective: Train Club leadership and Chaplains to behave efficiently during crises.

Phase	**Action**
Preparation	Review emergency contacts, crash-scene responsibilities, leadership brief.
Simulation	Conduct a mock accident drill: one casualty, one panic, one bystander.

Chaplain's Role	Stabilize emotion, support, SAA, manage crowd, initiate check-up.
Debrief	Analyze time, communication clarity, emotional control.

Run quarterly. Drills save lives and reputations.

Reflection

"The hardest runs are the ones with an empty seat. The Chaplain rides that space — between what was and what still must be. Every time he helps a brother through darkness, the patch shines a little brighter."

End-of-Chapter Summary

- Crisis ministry equals calm ministry.
- Early recognition prevents tragedy.
- Presence is stronger than preaching.
- Memorials heal by giving sorrow direction.
- Self-care is mandatory, not selfish.

🏍 CHAPTER EIGHT
Rituals, Ceremonies, and Sacred Traditions: Honoring the Spirit of the Club

"Ritual is memory in motion. Every tradition we keep says to the world, 'We haven't forgotten who we are."

The Purpose of Ritual

Armies, navies, congregations, and clubs all discovered the same truth:
When a group stops recognizing its milestones, morale dies quietly.

Rituals feed continuity; they turn events into tradition.
For a Motorcycle Club, ceremony ties together freedom and discipline, individuality and unity.
- A simple bike blessing before a season reminds riders they ride for something bigger.
- A moment of silence makes loss meaningful instead of random.
- An initiation transforms newcomers into members of a living story.

The Chaplain serves as **custodian of meaning**—the one who ensures every ritual, from memorial to meeting prayer, carries respect and authenticity.

The DNA of MC Ritual

1. **Authenticity over Formality.** Say a few true words well instead of many hollow ones.
2. **Symbol over Sermon.** Engines, patches, candles, coins—objects carry power when used intentionally.
3. **Unity over Uniformity.** Each Club's flavor is different; ceremonies should reflect that.
4. **Respect over Religion.** The Chaplain honors all beliefs by building language around loyalty, memory, and gratitude.

"You're not performing church; you're performing brotherhood."

Core Traditions and How to Lead Them

1. Blessing of the Bikes

- **Purpose:** Seek safe miles and mutual respect before riding season or major run.
- **Tone:** Optimistic, reflective, brief (2–3 minutes).
- **Structure:**
  1. Circle formation around bikes.
  2. Chaplain's words of unity and safety.
  3. Optional symbolic act – sprinkling water/oil, touching handlebars, or shared handshake.
  4. Closing – Engines start simultaneously; thunder becomes the amen.

2. Induction or Prospect Patch Presentation

- **Purpose:** Mark the transformation from probationary status to full patch brother in good standing.

- **Action:** Chaplain speaks briefly on responsibility, loyalty, and humility.
- **Example Line: >** "This patch isn't given for perfection—it's earned through endurance. Wear it knowing it represents everyone who stood where you stand tonight, all who came before you and those who will come after."
- **Present patch;** followed by President's handshake / hug and group salute.

3. Club Anniversary or Charter Dedication

- **Purpose:** Reaffirm identity, thank families, and renew commitment.
- **Structure:** Flag or color ceremony, reading of charter lines or original oath, short Chaplain reflection, collective toast or engine salute.
- **Tip: Display relics**—first patch, tools, photos—to remind members of roots.

4. Memorial Run or Remembrance Night

- Blend of military precision and biker heart.
- **Preparation:** List fallen members, gather family pictures or bikes, plan route through meaningful places.
- **During:** Chaplain reads names, brief reflection, one-minute silence, "Rev-Salute."
- **After:** Open floor: "Stories of the Road." Everyone allowed one short memory—keeps grief communal.

5. Farewell Ride / Last Ride Ceremony

Already detailed earlier, but Note here: - Coordinate with family, law enforcement, and Clubs on route safety.
- Bring water, tissues, and patience—grief rides slower than schedules.

- End with Chaplain's final words: > "From the earth to the wind, from silence to throttle—ride free, brother."

6. Blessing Before a Major Run

Before long-distance or risk-heavy journeys: - Quick lineup, helmets off.
- Chaplain states reason for ride + asks for clear weather, calm heads, wise hearts.
- Ends with: > "Check your tire pressure, your temper, and your trust. Let's roll."

Creating New Traditions

Clubs evolve—fresh ceremonies keep culture alive.
Examples:
- **Family Appreciation Night.** Recognize partners who hold the home front.
- **New Veteran Welcome.** Honor service without military hierarchy overshadowing the patch.
- **Community Service Blessing.** Before charity events, dedicate efforts to shared good.

Steps to craft a new ritual:

1. Define the why (purpose).
2. Choose a symbol (badge, candle, road, etc.).
3. Set a flow (opening, act, closing).
4. Write words – plain, short, heartfelt.
5. Perform and record (photolog or minutes so future Chaplains can repeat).

Symbolism Toolbox

Symbol	**Meaning in MC Context**	**Usage**
Engine Rev	Power + Presence = Life	Salute, memorial closing
Candle / Light	Reflection, memory	Vigils, commemorations
Coin / Patch	Commitment, loyalty	Awards, remembrances
Bell	Time, passage	Moment of silence markers
Road Sand / Dust	Journey, authenticity	Sprinkle at burials or dedications
Gloves on Bike Seat	Absence, remembrance	Display at memorial
Circle Formation	Unity, equality	Any major ceremony position

Each object should tell a story; don't use props you can't explain.

Tone and Delivery

The Chaplain's voice defines the ceremony's personality. Follow the three C's:

- **Calm:** Low, deliberate tone. Silence beats shouting.
- **Clear:** Every word purposeful; no filler.
- **Consistent:** Ceremonial demeanor—sober but warm—creates trust.

Format notes:
- Stand centered but not superior; you represent, not command.
- Eye contact halfway between the flag and the people—symbolizing loyalty to both.
- Keep ceremonies under 10 minutes unless specific ritual calls for longer.

Handling Inter-Club Ceremonies

When multiple Clubs attend:

- Consult all presidents beforehand regarding protocol and flag order.
- Speak from club neutral position—Chaplain of the Brotherhood, not one patch.
- Avoid divisive symbols or language.
- End with unifying message: > "Different colors, same road."

Preserving Tradition

Record each major ritual: date, location, attendance, key lines spoken.
Compile into a **Club Ritual Logbook**.
Future Chaplains can draw from it, ensuring continuity when leadership changes.

Train prospects on ceremonial respect: helmets and hats off, engines cut, phones silent, no talking.

Tradition doesn't trap progress; it gives progress roots.

Dragon's Field Reflection

"Every patch carries memory. When a Chaplain speaks over bikes and brothers, he's not giving orders—he's giving history a heartbeat."

Exercise – Ceremony Design Workshop

Conduct during leadership or regional Chaplain gatherings:

1. Divide attendees into small groups.
2. Assign them ceremony types (Memorial, Blessing, Initiation...).
3. Each group crafts an outline with purpose, flow, props, and sample words.
4. Perform live; discuss tone and authenticity.
5. Collect all samples into shared Ritual Manual for chapters.

Reflection

"The Club's spirit lives in its rituals. Engines stop, then thunder again, reminding us that endings and beginnings sound the same. A Chaplain ensures neither is ever empty."

End-of-Chapter Summary

- Rituals turn routine into remembrance.
- Keep ceremonies short + sincere.
- Use symbols riders understand.
- Adapt military structure to Club soul.
- Record and train to preserve tradition.

◊◊◊

🏍 CHAPTER NINE
The Chaplain's Toolkit:
Prayers, Reflections, and Field Resources

"When the moment hits, you won't have time to write a speech. That's why you build the toolkit before you roll."

Purpose of the Toolkit

This chapter isn't theory — it's your grab-bag of words and actions for the road, the meeting hall, or the memorial field.
Every entry can be read verbatim or changed to fit the Club's tone. Nothing here represents one religion; every line speaks to loyalty, gratitude, courage, and humility — the universal backbone of the biker spirit.

1. Field Reflections

Short readings the Chaplain can use to open or close rides, meetings, or quiet moments.

Reflection A – The Road and the Brotherhood

"Every road begins with a choice: ride alone or ride together. We choose together, because miles mean nothing without the ones who ride beside us. May the road be clear, the hearts steady, and the brotherhood unbroken."

Reflection B – Strength and Humility

"Power without mercy wrecks anything it touches. Let strength serve loyalty, and humility steer both. In that balance lives the courage that keeps a Club alive."

Reflection C – Gratitude on the Run

"For every mile behind us and every one still waiting, we give thanks — not to luck, but to loyalty, discipline, and the patience of those who keep the home fires burning."

Reflection D – The Fall and the Rise

"Everyone goes down eventually — a crash, a failure, a heartbreak. But the ride isn't over until we stay down. Brothers fall, brothers lift. That's the only rule that matters."

2. Quick Blessings

These can be recited or paraphrased in less than a minute — perfect for gatherings, rides, or hospital visits.

Setting	**Sample Blessing Text**
Before a Run	"May our bikes stay strong, our reflexes sharp, and our tempers cool. Let today's miles remind us that freedom costs awareness. Ride safe and true."
Club Meeting Opening	"Grant us clear heads, tight tongues, and loyal hearts. May everything we say here

	strengthen, not split, our brotherhood."
Club Meeting Closing	"We came as many voices; we leave as one spirit. Respect earned, respect kept. Until next time — ride steady."
Hospital Visit	"Brother, your body's resting but your spirit's still roaring. Heal, rebuild, return stronger. The road will wait."
Memorial Moment	"We honor the miles you gave us and the peace you found. Ride free now, and watch over your family of steel and blood below."

(Each can be delivered solo or followed by a short pause for personal additions.)

3. Readings for Ceremonies

A. Oath of Brotherhood Renewal

"We remember why we wear these colors: to prove loyalty through action, to protect what we love without compromise, and to live wide open until the end of our road. Together we renew it, here and now."

B. Grief and Strength

"Loss hits hardest in the quiet moments when engines are cold. Yet every start-up tomorrow will carry a piece of those we lost. They live in the roar, in the wind, and in the stories we keep telling."

C. Unity Among Clubs

"Different patches, same road. Different stories, same heartbeat. Respect crosses all colors; the asphalt doesn't care which logo leads — only that we ride with honor."

4. Personal Morning Ritual for the Chaplain

Borrowing from naval watch preparations, done in private before duties begin.

1. **Center.** Sit still 30 seconds; breathe deep.
2. **Affirm.** Whisper: *"I serve by presence, not position."*
3. **Prepare.** Glove check, patch check, heart check.
4. **Commit.** Visualize being calm under pressure today.
5. **Ride.** Move with purpose — conversations today may carry unseen importance.

5. Evening Decompression Reflection

Used to close the day or a long ride.

"Engines cool, silence settles, and every mile becomes memory. What did I give today? What did I learn? Who needs a word from me tomorrow? May my rest sharpen my service."

Write short notes afterward in your Field Journal: people to check on, lessons learned, gratitude list.

6. Ready Phrases for Difficult Moments

Situation	Anchor Phrase
After a crash (scene secure)	"You're not alone, brother. We've got you."
Conflict deescalation	"Let's pause — respect deserves a second to breathe."
Grief or funeral	"We mourn because love mattered. That's worth every tear."
Private counsel	"Tell it straight; I don't judge, I listen."
Leadership advice	"Boss, here's what the heart of the Club is feeling right now."

7. Tools & Contacts to Keep Handy

Emergency Numbers

- Local 911 or regional equivalent
- Nearest hospital ER address
- Veterans Crisis Hotline or National Suicide Prevention Line (number insertable per country)
- Designated Club Legal Advisor
- Next-of-kin contact list (kept secure with president)

Supplies Checklist

- Updated Field Journal
- Portable Light / Candle

- Spare Pens and Small Paper Cards
- Club Coins and Memorial Tokens
- Business cards of trusted counselors
- Water, snacks, basic first-aid
- Phone charger / portable battery

Reference Reminders

- Chaplains' Code Four (**Care**, **Facilitate**, **Provide**, **Advise**)
- Confidentiality Promise - quoted line: *"What's shared in faith stays protected by honor."*
- Crisis Steps Formula: **Assess** → **Stabilize** → **Connect** → **Follow-up**.

Dragon's Note to Field Chaplains

"These aren't magic words; they're starting points. A Chaplain's real power is listening first, speaking second, and riding back tomorrow to prove he meant it."

8. Exercise – Quick-Draw Drill

Objective: Train new Chaplains to deliver calm words under pressure.

Instructions:
- Leadership or senior Chaplain calls out a random scenario: injury, argument, loss, blessing, or media request.
- Trainee
has 30 seconds to deliver an authentic 30-second response.
- Feedback focus: tone, brevity, sincerity, presence.

Run monthly; compile strongest phrases into shared chapter handbook.

Reflection

"Wisdom packs light. A few true lines, a calm touch, and the will to show up—that's all a Chaplain ever really needs in his toolkit."

End-of-Chapter Summary

- Prepare before the crisis; write, edit, memorize short reflections.
- Keep your toolkit literal and spiritual.
- Focus each phrase on unity, respect, courage, and healing.
- Revise yearly as the Club and season change.

🏍 CHAPTER Ten
Mentorship and Legacy:
Training the Next Generation of MC Chaplains

"What we teach outlives what we ride."

The Responsibility of Continuity

Every seasoned Chaplain eventually trades firsts for repeats—first accident, first funeral, first crisis. The experience you gain doesn't belong only to you; it belongs to the longevity of the patch.

A true leader doesn't hoard knowledge; he passes it on polished by experience and scar tissue. Mentorship turns moments into methods.

As *The Navy Chaplain's Manual* puts it, *"The effectiveness of the corps depends on the training of its future."* The same applies here: the effectiveness of the Brotherhood's Soul-Corps depends on how you raise your replacements.

The Mission of Mentorship

Goal: develop competent, trusted Chaplains who can lead spiritually, emotionally, and practically without losing the Club's culture or edge.

Mentorship accomplishes three things:

1. **Preservation:** passing on the ethics and rituals established through this handbook.
2. **Preparation:** training new Chaplains before crisis, not after appointment.

3. **Protection:** safeguarding continuity when leadership rotates or members move on.

"If the next Chaplain needs to ask how to handle a funeral, the last one failed to prepare him."

Identifying Future Chaplains

Look for *quiet steadiness*, not loud charisma.

Indicators:

- Respected by all ranks, trusted by leadership.
- Can keep a secret and a schedule.
- Balances emotion with discipline.
- Already serves informally—comforting, mediating, showing up.
- Reads, listens, learns without ego.

When such a person appears, invest time early. Bring him alongside during runs, meetings, and ceremonies. Let him observe before he officiates.

The Mentorship Cycle

Stage	Description	Outcome
Observation	Shadowing senior Chaplain during ceremonies, counseling, ride-outs.	Learner understands tone and procedure.
Assisted Participation	Junior delivers small portions—reading reflection, starting a blessing, helping at hospital visits.	Skill building with guidance.
Independent Action	Junior handles full duty while senior stands back.	Confidence, real-time correction afterward.
Evaluation & Feedback	Honest debrief — what went well, what to sharpen.	Growth without humiliation.

Certification & Commissioning	Formal recognition by leadership or regional Chaplain's council.	Continuity and pride cemented.

Repeat annually; mentorship never truly ends.

Building a Chaplain's Network

Just as the Navy maintains a "community of practice," MC Chaplains build regional alliances:

- Share ceremony scripts, training drills, and resource lists.
- Coordinate joint memorial rides.
- Support each other after line-of-duty trauma.

A networked Chaplain never burns out; someone else always understands the burden.

The Archives of Experience

Create and maintain a Chaplain's Legacy Binder:

- Short personal reflections on incidents — lessons learned.
- Copies of ceremonies, blessings, and templates used.
- Photos, programs, obituaries (with permissions).
- Contact lists for community partners.
- Annual moral health summaries for the Club.

Store it in the Club's archive locker or digital drive. It becomes the institutional memory of the soul, a gift to the next generation.

Discipleship vs Duplication

Mentoring doesn't mean cloning yourself. Each new Chaplain will bring his own style, faith expression, or generational flavor. The goal is not preservation of personality; it's preservation of principle. Teach **what must never change**:

1. Confidentiality.
2. Integrity of the Code.
3. Respect across belief systems.
4. Calm during conflict.
5. Commitment to service before status.

Everything else—phrasing, rituals, tone—can evolve.

Succession Planning

Prepare the line of succession before it's needed.

When you sense your term ending:

- Inform leadership privately.
- Nominate and train a successor early.
- Conduct formal hand-off during a meeting or ceremony; read the Chaplain's Oath anew together.
- Present symbols — field kit, coin, or logbook — to transfer responsibility with dignity.

"The soul of the Club doesn't retire; it is re-enlisted with every new Chaplain."

Dragon's Mentorship Tip

"Train your shadow as if you'll vanish tomorrow. That's how you make sure the light keeps following the road."

Exercise – Mentor's Table

Once each quarter, gather Chaplains and officers.

- Each presents a scenario recently faced and how it was handled.
- Group discusses alternate actions, lessons learned, and psychological cues.
- Record highlights in the Legacy Binder under "Mentor's Table Notes."

This becomes living doctrine—practical street ethics refined over time.

Reflection

"Leadership ends; influence echoes.
A Chaplain's true promotion is when another steps up already ready."

End-of-Chapter Summary

- Identify steady hearts early.
- Mentor through observation, participation, and feedback.
- Network regionally for resilience.
- Record and pass on wisdom.
- Plan succession intentionally; legacy doesn't happen by accident.

◊◊◊

🏍 CHAPTER Eleven
Legacy of the Chaplain:
Remembrance, Honor, and the Final Run

"Every road ends in horizon, but a Chaplain's duty never finishes — it just changes terrain."

The Echo of Service

One day, the miles will stop counting.
The keys will hang in silence.
Another Chaplain will take your seat, carrying the same field kit you once packed, the same prayers you once spoke.
That's what legacy means — service beyond self, presence that keeps guiding after your last ride.

From the first Guardians of the Cloak to the sailors' chapels deep beneath the waves, to the leather-clad brothers gathered around a fire, one line remains unbroken: *men and women who stand for others when the noise dies down.*

Legacy is not built in speeches.
It lives in examples that outlast explanation.

Why Legacy Matters

The President leads the Club's direction, the Sergeant-at-Arms guards its order, but the Chaplain guards its memory.
When you step away, the next generation should still feel your influence embedded in the culture — in how brothers settle

arguments, in how they speak the names of the fallen, in how they ride with dignity.

Legacy is the soul's afterimage.
It appears whenever your example gets copied unconsciously.

Remembrance

Memorials and rituals aren't about the dead; they are for the living. They remind us that loyalty and love are stronger than distance.

The Chaplain ensures that those memories never fade into bar stories.

- Keep a **Book of the Fallen** — name, date, photograph, and a line from each life.
- Maintain anniversary traditions — bell tolls, candle runs, or ride-outs in silence.
- When you speak their names, do it with the weight of brotherhood, not theatrics.
  Each time you lead that ritual right, you teach the Club how to face loss with strength.

It's not just remembrance — it's **continuity of character**.

Honor

Honor is more than ceremony; it's posture toward the world.
A Chaplain's posture teaches that respecting others never lowers our pride; it raises our reputation.

To *honor* is:

- to ride clean, even when no one's looking.
- to speak straight, even when it costs.

- to uphold protocol with humility, not arrogance.
- to see value in every patch, every color, every soul who shares the road.

Every time the Club acts with honor, the Chaplain's influence is showing — even if his name is never said.

The Final Run

Someday your own name will join the Book of the Fallen.
Plan for that day with the calm of a road captain charting one last route.

Write your instructions: where your patch goes, what words you want spoken, who carries the flag or coin.
But remember: you can't script brotherhood — you can only inspire it in advance.
If you've lived this handbook, your ceremony will happen naturally, without rehearsal.
The Club will know exactly how to honor you because you showed them how to honor others.

"When the road calls my name, bury the sermon, not the standard. Keep the throttle steady, keep the faith strong, and keep each other standing."

Legacy in Motion

Legacy doesn't sit in archives; it moves on two wheels.
Each new Chaplain is a continuation, not a replacement.

Pass on three things:

1. **Your stories –** because lessons hide inside laughter and mistakes.
2. **Your rituals –** because structure outlives emotion.
3. **Your calm –** because peace is the hardest thing to replace.

The generation that comes next should feel your guidance not as a shadow but as sunlight on their own road.

Dragon's Final Note

"Leadership ends; influence rides forever.
When your engine goes silent, may your brothers still hear the rhythm of your example echo through theirs."

Closing Reflection —

"The Road Without End"

We all arrive at dusk one day, and when that time comes, the question won't be how far we rode, but how many found direction because we did.

To every future Chaplain, remember:
you're not keeping a religion alive — you're keeping a brotherhood human.

Ride well, serve humbly, speak gently,
and the road ahead will always clear for those following in your mirrors.

End of Manuscript Closing

"Honor. Respect. Loyalty. Faith.
The road continues."

Honorably yours

Black Dragon
Former National President
Former National Enforcer
Former East Coast Regional President
Founder Black Sabbath MC Goddesses of the Cross
Founder Black Sabbath MC Sisters of the Cross
Founder/President/Original 7 Atlanta Chapter
Lifer
Mighty Black Sabbath MC Nation
A Breed Apart
BSFFBS
Since 1974 and still strong…………..///

End of Book

🏍 Glossary

A

Accountability – The habit of owning actions and consequences without excuse; a pillar of leadership and morality for Chaplains.

After-Action Review (AAR) – Post-event reflection borrowed from the military; used here for debriefing ceremonies, crises, or training exercises.

Allegiance, Dual – The Chaplain's simultaneous loyalty to Club leadership and to conscience — supporting both without betraying either.

B

Backbone, Moral – The ethical spine of the Club; its shared courage, discipline, and respect that hold everything upright.

Bible (B-Series) – The established style of John E. "Black Dragon" Bunch II's manuals; straight-talk field books on MC leadership.

Blessing of the Bikes – Traditional ceremony of asking protection and purpose for riders and machines at the start of a season or journey.

Bridge Reflection – Self-assessment page between chapters, reminding Chaplains to maintain personal balance before leading others.

Brotherhood – The bond between members forged through shared miles, loyalty, and respect — the foundation of all MC culture.

C

Capella / Chapel – Original Latin for "little cloak"; where the relic of Saint Martin's cloak (*cappa*) was kept — birthplace of the word *chaplain*.

Chaplain – From Latin *cappellanus*, "guardian of the cloak." In MC life, a member entrusted with the spiritual and moral welfare of the Club.

Chaplain's Code Four – The fourfold duty system: Care, Facilitate, Provide, Advise.

Chaplain's Field Kit – Practical and symbolic collection of gear, notes, and tools a Chaplain carries for ceremonies or crises.

Chain of Command – The leadership hierarchy within a Club. The Chaplain respects it but speaks truth across it when conscience demands.

Code – Unwritten moral rules governing behavior, conduct, and loyalty inside every MC; "the soul behind the bylaws."

Confidential Communication – Private conversation given to the Chaplain in trust; sacred information never to be shared without clear danger to life or Club integrity.

D

Discipline – The structure and self-control that keeps freedom functional; cornerstone of both military and Club order.

Dual Allegiance – The Chaplain's balancing act between serving leadership and serving all members equally.

E

Ethos – The guiding moral spirit or character of a group; what a combination of Spirit, Discipline, and Code creates.

F

Field Journal – Chaplain's notebook for event logs, ceremonies, or reflections. Confidential; a written moral compass.

Final Run – The symbolic last ride honoring a fallen rider; also, the Chaplain's eventual passage to the next road.

H

Honor – Personal integrity expressed through consistent right action, especially when no one is watching.

L

Legacy Binder – Archive maintained by the Chaplain documenting ceremonies, memorials, and lessons for future Chaplains.

Loyalty Vertical / Horizontal – Vertical: obedience up the chain; Horizontal: compassion across the brotherhood. The Chaplain balances both.

M

Mentor's Table – Periodic gathering of Chaplains and officers to share case studies and lessons; keeps doctrine alive and field-tested.

Ministry of Presence – Core concept from military chaplaincy; simply *being there* with calm and empathy rather than preaching.

Moral Compass – The inner sense of right and wrong guiding decisions; a Chaplain's unissued weapon.

N

Neutral Ground – Emotional and political zone the Chaplain occupies to mediate conflict without side-taking.

O

Oath, Chaplain's – Formal vow during commissioning, promising confidentiality, courage, and service beyond self.

P

Patch – The Club's emblem worn on a rider's vest; represents identity, loyalty, and earned status. For a Chaplain, it also symbolizes stewardship of the brotherhood's spirit.

Presence Ministry – Synonym for *ministry of presence*. See M.

R

Ride Out Drill – Annual training exercise for Chaplains simulating stress scenarios on the road; field skills test.

Rituals – Symbolic acts—funerals, blessings, memorials—that express and preserve a Club's values.

S

Sacred Trust – The unspoken contract between Chaplain and Club ensuring privacy, respect, and reliability.

Serenity – Calm composure maintained under pressure; the visible mark of a tested Chaplain.

Spirit – The living energy of the Club — morale, brotherhood, respect — protected by the Chaplain.

Succession Plan – Process by which an outgoing Chaplain trains and hands off duties to his successor.

T

Table Top Drill – Discussion-based scenario training used to prepare Chaplains for field crises.

Trust Bridge – Relationship of confidence between a Chaplain and leadership or membership, maintained entirely through reliability.

W

Walk the Example – To let behavior speak louder than any sermon; daily embodiment of the Chaplain's oath.

Wind Therapy – The healing power many riders find in the simple act of riding; one of the Chaplain's tools for recovery and reflection.

"Know the words and you'll understand the world they describe.
Live the meaning and the world will understand you."

— Black Dragon

🏍 Bibliography

Compiled by John E. "Black Dragon" Bunch II
(All works referenced for concept development, training methodology, or historical background.)

Primary Military and Chaplaincy References

- Frazier, John B.
  The Navy Chaplain's Manual. Department of the Navy, Naval Chaplain's Corps, Washington D.C.

- Department of the Navy. *SECNAV Instruction 1730.10A — Religious Ministry within the Department of the Navy and the Navy Chaplain Corps Program.*

- Chief of Chaplains Office.
  *CHC *Chaplains Guide to Professional Naval Chaplaincy (PNC).*

- mPact Churches International.
  Military Chaplain Handbook (2023 Revision).

- U.S. Army Training and Doctrine Command.
  Field Manual 1-05: Religious Support in Unified Land Operations. Headquarters, Department of the Army.

- Chaplain Corps College, U.S. Navy.
  CHC Final: Professional Naval Chaplaincy Core Competencies. Newport, RI.

- U.S. Air Force Chaplain Corps.
  The Chaplain Mentoring Program Guide. Department of the Air Force.

Leadership, Ethics, and Historical Works

- Sun Tzu.
  The Art of War. Trans. Lionel Giles. Modern Library Classics.

- Aurelius, Marcus.
  Meditations. Trans. Gregory Hays. Modern Library.

- Willink, Jocko & Babin, Leif.
  Extreme Ownership: How U.S. Navy SEALs Lead and Win. St. Martin's Press, 2015.

- Covey, Stephen R.
  The 7 Habits of Highly Effective People. Free Press, 1989.

- Nouwen, Henri.
  The Wounded Healer: Ministry in Contemporary Society. Ima ge Books, 1979.

- Wright, H. Norman.
  Crisis Counseling: A Guide for Pastors and Professionals. Reg al Books, 1985.

- Department of Defense. *Ethical Leadership Field Guide – Character Counts in DoD.*

Motorcycle Club Culture and Leadership

- Bunch II, John E. "Black Dragon."
  "Prospect's Bible: How to Prospect for a Traditional, Law Abiding Motorcycle Club." Bunch Publishing/Bunch Media Group.

- *Bunch II, John E. "Black Dragon."*
  "MC Public Relations Officer's Manual: Modern MC Communications." Bunch Publishing/Bunch Media Group

- *Bunch II, John E. "Black Dragon." "Sergeant-at-Arms Bible: Soldier Sergeant of the MC"* Bunch Publishing/Bunch Media Group
- *Bunch II, John E. "Black Dragon." "President's Bible Chronicle I: Principles of Motorcycle Club Leadership."* Bunch Publishing/Bunch Media Group
- *Bunch II, John E. "Black Dragon." "Robert's Rules for Motorcycle Clubs: Running Church the Right Way"* Bunch Publishing/Bunch Media Group
- *Bunch II, John E. "Black Dragon." "Social Clubs Bible: Revival of the Women's Social Club Movement.* Bunch Publishing/Bunch Media Group
- *Bunch II, John E. "Black Dragon." "Prospect's Bible for Women's Motorcycle Clubs."* Bunch Publishing/Bunch Media Group
- *Bunch II, John E. "Black Dragon." "Motorcycle Club Protocol 101: The Social Construct of Motorcycle Club Life, Rules, Traditions, History, Politics and Modus Operandi"* Bunch Publishing/Bunch Media Group
- *Bunch II, John E. "Black Dragon." "The Art of War for Motorcycle Clubs."* Bunch Publishing/Bunch Media Group

Faith and Inter-Religious Studies

- Military Chaplains Association of the USA.
  Handbook of Faiths for Armed Forces Chaplaincy. Washingto
  n D.C.

- Parrinder, Geoffrey.
  World Religions: From Ancient History to Present.
  Facts on File, 2000.

- The Interfaith Network.
  World Scripture and the Teachings of Peace.
  Universal Peace Federation.

Cultural and Psychological Resources

- American Veterans Association.
  PTSD and Trauma Recovery Handbook for Support Workers.
  Veterans Press, 2021.

- U.S. Department of Veterans Affairs.
  VA Chaplains Resource Manual. Office of Patient
  Centered Care & Cultural Transformation, 2019.

Historical and Inspirational Sources

- Louth, Andrew.
  The Origins of the Christian Chaplains and Saint
  Martin of Tours. Cambridge University Press, 1986.

- MacCulloch, Diarmaid.
  A History of Christianity. Penguin Books, 2009.

Media and Digital Sources

- Black Dragon Biker TV. (YouTube channel). Segments on MC leadership and Club Ethics, 2016-present.
- U.S. Navy Chaplain Corps Online Archive. https://www.navy.mil/chaplaincorps (accessed March 2024).
- mPact Churches Resource Portal. https://www.mpactglobal.org (training materials 2020–2023).

Unpublished & Personal Field Materials

- Field notes, diaries, and ceremonial logs maintained by John E. "Black Dragon" Bunch II during ten years in the Silent Service and over two decades of MC leadership.
- Oral interviews with regional MC Chaplain Officers (United States & U.K., 2022–2024).

"Books preserve knowledge; roads prove it. Between the two lives the Chaplain." — *Black Dragon*

◊◊◊

🏍 How to Use This Handbook in the Field

"A book is just paper until it rides with you."
— Black Dragon

This manual was built to work, not just to read.
Treat it the way a Marine treats a field guide or a prospect treats his notebook — tool first, trophy second.

1. Carry It, Don't Shelf It

- Keep a field copy with you — in the clubhouse office, saddlebag, or backpack.
- Plastic-sleeve or laminate the most-used pages: Field Kit list, Crisis Protocol, Blessings, Code Four.
- Mark your personal additions and favorite readings — this book should look lived-in.

2. Customize for Your Club

Every Club has its own rhythm.
Add your patch name to ceremonies. Adapt prayers to your language. Replace "amen" with your own closing salute.
Never change the principles. Honor, confidentiality, service, presence — those stay constant.

3. Train With It

- Use the Scenario-Based Drills and Ride-Out Exercises as meeting devotionals or training nights.
- Assign sections for prospects or assistant Chaplains to study; quiz them on crisis sequence.
- Record after-action notes directly in the margins.

4. Reference Fast

Use the Quick-Reference Index and color tabs for:

- *Ceremonies & Rituals*
- *Crisis Response Plan*
- *Training Drills*
- *Chaplain's Oath & Commissioning*

> *"If time is short and tension high, these pages replace hesitation with action."*
> *— Black Dragon*

5. Expand the Legacy

When you create a new reading, ritual, or reflection that works, add it to your Legacy Binder and share it through your regional Chaplain network.
Every update keeps the handbook alive and the brotherhood evolving.

6. Field Maintenance

Wipe off grease, tape the torn pages, keep a second copy in the clubhouse safe.
A scarred book is a used book, and a used book saves time when lives or tempers hang in the balance.

"Read softly, act decisively, ride faithfully.
This handbook isn't just yours — it belongs to the next Chaplain waiting for an example."

🏍 Appendix I
Spiritual Leadership in the 1%er World

"To lead where rules don't reach, a Chaplain must live by a higher code inside himself."
— Black Dragon

Introduction: Faith in a World of Outlaws

Inside traditional motorcycle club culture, especially among 1%er clubs, spirituality doesn't always wear a cross, a collar, or a Sunday suit.

In this world, *faith* is measured by **loyalty, integrity, and courage under heat** — not by sermons.

The 1%er universe is built on independence and defiance.
Each patch defends its freedom from outside interference — including organized religion.

That doesn't mean it rejects faith; it means it **defines faith differently**: as the discipline to live and die by one's chosen code. Spiritual leadership here requires a Chaplain who understands both the *language of the street* and the *architecture of the heart*.

1. Understanding the Environment

1%ers are **paramilitary, family, and tribe** rolled into one.
Their faith expression exists in:

- honor between brothers,

- loyalty to lineage,
- and silence about internal matters.

A Chaplain entering this world walks a narrow line between **credibility and curiosity**. You earn trust not by quoting scripture but by proving you understand *respect, risk, and retaliation.*

Core Truths

- **Trust precedes listening.** No one will hear your message until they believe you bleed the same road.
- **Presence outweighs preaching.** You show care by showing up — not showing off.
- **Neutrality equals survival.** Never play politics between clubs, charters, or factions.
- **Confidentiality is sacred.** What you hear stays locked, unless life is in danger.

2. Building Credibility as a 1%er Chaplain

1. **Be a Real Brother First.**
    - Earn your patch; pay your dues. Spiritual authority grows from earned equity, not appointment.
2. **Live the Code Without Compromise.**
    - Every deed must match your counsel. Hypocrisy gets you isolated fast.
3. **Show Skill and Grit.**
    - Ride the miles, share the work, show up during confrontation. Soft men get no hearing.
4. **Speak Plain, Speak Short.**
    - One sentence of truth carries more than an hour of talk.
5. **Respect the Hierarchy but Guard the Spirit.**

    - You answer to leadership, but your authority flows from quiet conviction.

Once you've proved you understand the road, even hardened men open their doors to the language of peace.

3. Faith Without Religion

In outlaw circles, "religion" often means judgment and hypocrisy. But **spiritual leadership**— integrity, forgiveness, gratitude, redemption — translates to every man alive.
A skilled Chaplain uses **universal language**:

- Instead of "pray," say *"take a moment of respect."*
- Instead of "God bless," use *"may your road stay clear and your word stay strong."*
- Instead of quoting texts, draw from experience: *"I've seen mercy save more men than bullets."*

"Your calm is your cathedral; your example is your sermon."

Speak from authenticity, not authority.

4. The Role of Ritual in the 1%er World

Even the roughest charters have rituals: patching ceremonies, memorial rides, run blessings, "moment of silence" traditions. These are sacred in their own right.
The Chaplain's job:

- Protect these ceremonies from mockery or outside intrusion.
- Remind the Club that ritual unites the tribe.
- Keep ceremonies concise and masculine — strength without sentimentality.

- Ensure symbols retain true meaning: the patch, the bell, the handshake, the last ride.

Ritual holds the line where law doesn't.

5. Moral Compass in a Code-Run Culture

The 1%er community's moral system isn't lawless — it's **honor-based**.

A Chaplain operates like an internal compass:

- Encourage restraint before violence when pride threatens peace.
- Counsel brothers to maintain collective reputation; the Club lives or dies by it.
- Remind leadership that mercy can sometimes save more power than fear.
- Uphold loyalty without excusing self-destruction.

The Rule of Three Questions

Before you act or speak:

1. Would this strengthen the **Brotherhood**?
2. Would it preserve our **Honor**?
3. Would I be proud if it was retold after I'm gone?
   If any answer is *no*, re-route the decision.

6. Dealing with Outside World Pressure

1%er Chaplains often act as diplomats during legal trouble, public scrutiny, or community misunderstandings.
Key tips:

- Never speak to law enforcement or media without permission.
- When authorized, project calm, rational representation — your demeanor is the Club's first line of defense.
- Build quiet community respect through charity, mentorship, or veteran outreach.
  Good deeds don't erase outlaw roots; they redefine what "outlaw" can mean.

7. When Violence Calls

No Chaplain glorifies violence, yet refusing to recognize its presence would be naïve.
If violence erupts:

- Protect lives first, loyalty second.
- De-escalate where possible: calm voice, clear movements, visible respect.
- After the dust settles, guide reconciliation — not justification.
- Remember : a brother's life lost to rage is one sermon you'll preach forever.

8. The Quiet Mission

The outlaw world respects strength, but its heart aches for peace like any other.
The Chaplain's mission isn't to reform the lifestyle; it's to **bring light into dark corners** without dulling anyone's edge.

Practical ways:

- One-on-one garage talks.
- Small reflection nights after heavy runs.
- Text messages of loyalty and care.
- Visiting brothers in lockup or hospitals.

These acts speak louder than pulpits and last longer than rules.

9. Legacy of the 1%er Chaplain
You represent an elite few — those who bridge worlds:

- **Between freedom and faith,**
- **between rebellion and reason,**
- **between loyalty and love.**

Your success isn't measured by converts but by **how many men make wiser choices because you stood nearby.**

"The outlaw world doesn't need preaching; it needs proof. Be that proof."

Closing Reflection

They call themselves the one percent because they live outside the line. A true Chaplain works that edge — not to drag them inside, but to keep them from falling off. If you can do that with grace and grit, you'll change more hearts than sermons ever could.

◊◊◊

Appendix II
The Chaplain's Personal Habits and Conduct from the Navy Chaplain's Manual 1917 by John B. Frazier first Chief of Chaplains of the Navy

It would be difficult to find a place where one's personal habits are subject to closer scrutiny or are more constantly on exhibition than in the cramped quarters of a man-of-war. A few weeks of this intimate association are sufficient to publish to all on board what a man does and is. Habits that in civil life might not make one particularly objectionable are here so magnified by the intimacy of their touch as to make one who on shore might be a fairly decent fellow anything but a desirable ship-mate. To be a gentleman in the usual acceptation of that term is hardly a sufficient criterion. In fact, a lot of things that are accepted without hesitancy on shore would not apply to life aboard ship. Many gentlemen in civil life do not bathe oftener than once a week. Some of them shave only when the beard becomes uncomfortable. Others neglect the hair-cut, and some no doubt are not familiar with the hygiene of the tooth-brush or the nail-brush. The failure to observe these sanitary laws may not materially interfere with their standing; but, while such neglect on board ship may be tolerated, it brands the guilty one as lacking the elements of decency.

No one likes to eat beside another whose awkward manipulation of his knife and fork endangers the clothing of his neighbor, and to have such manipulation accompanied by the musical disappearance of soup is enough to interfere very materially with the success of tone who has no other faults.

One's personal appearance is the first introduction one has to a stranger. The observing man who meets another for the first time formulates an opinion of him even before he grasps his hand or hears the sound of his greeting. With one glance he takes in his personal appearance, and though the opinion later may be changed, first impressions are lasting. Well shined shoes, clothes carefully brushed, and linen on which there is no grime, covering the person of a careful man, bespeaks an inward cleanliness that goes far toward establishing him in the good graces of one who meets him for the first time and toward maintaining his standing among those who know him well.

There are some habits and practices in other officers that are not considered objectionable, but which in a Chaplain are at least not becoming. These are mentioned not to set a standard for other men—for each must be his own judge—but because young chaplains have asked for information. It is a difficult fact, but a fact nevertheless, that a clergyman is not expected to live according to the standards set by the world. Like Caesar's wife, he must be above suspicion—not only aboard ship but on shore. He is the moral and religious "pace setter"; and when he, by "slowing up" through conformity to the ways of the world, forgets this fact, his influence as a moral and religious teacher ceases.

There are clergymen who play cards, but it is a question as to whether this practice has ever added anything commendable to the reputation of a single one. There are others who consider it not unbecoming to take an occasional drink of wine or other intoxicant, not habitually, but on occasions of ceremony. The practice is bad, and undoubtedly has resulted in destroying the influence for good of many men who otherwise were above reproach. One whose breath is tainted with that "which steals away the brain" is in no shape to preach temperance to another who, by reason of indulgence is on the downward way. One of the chief duties of a Chaplain is to uphold by precept and example the efforts of wise men to make and keep the Navy sober. Only those of us who have been in the Service under the old and the new regime are in a position to pass judgment on the wisdom of that law which forbids the use of introduction of intoxicants on board ship. Every officer who has the welfare of the Service at heart should thank God for the day when "booze was piped over the side" and pray that it may never return.

The temptation to indulge in the recital of questionable stories is peculiar to companies of men who live apart from what Dr. Johnson calls the "elegant and elevating influence of female friendship." Such stories may be good to raise a laugh, but they are not good for those who hear them, nor for the one who tells them. For a Chaplain so far to forget himself as to relate a vile or a lewd story is unpardonable, and while men may laugh, deep down in their hearts there is a sense of disgust.

How to conduct oneself in the midst of unaccustomed surroundings and conditions, that to a clergyman may be embarrassing, is a great big problem. The sense of adaptability in some men is such that from the very beginning they have no difficulty; but for most young chaplains the ordeal is extremely trying, and unless one carefully guards himself will result in driving him either into seclusion or indulgence in that which is not becoming. To avoid these extremes, one should remember that the day of the cloister and convent for men is past, that while a Christian is ordered not to be "of the world," nevertheless, in order to do a man's work, he must be in it. It is, therefore, his business to face difficult situations like a man, and to adapt himself to them in such a way that while not compromising his principles he may still not give offense. A ship is like a little city, and just as no citizen can regulate and order the life of another in that city, just so can no individual on board ship arbitrarily form and fashion the conduct of another. If your next-door [sic] neighbor gives a party to which you are not invited, and it does not meet with your approbation, being a gentleman you have no right, nor can you afford to refer to the slight or express your disapproval. The ship is the home not of one but of all, and all have equal rights, and so long as men do not think alike, so long will they not act alike. Accordingly, instead of dictating the policy of others, "act well your part," remembering that "there all the honor lies."

Appendix III Visiting the Sick and Imprisoned from the Navy Chaplain's Manual 1917 by John B. Frazier first Chief of Chaplains of the Navy

VISITING THE SICK AND IMPRISONED

This is seldom if ever a pleasant part of the Chaplain's duty. Nevertheless, it is one of great importance and will require great tact and good judgment if it is not to be made a mere matter of form. Sick people as a rule are oversensitive and prisoners are usually grouchy and unapproachable. The tendency on the part of both is to feel that "nobody cares." It is the business of the Chaplain to convince them that somebody "does care," and to do this he must be able to convey the fact without putting it into words.

The Sick Bay is under the immediate control of the Senior Surgeon. As a matter of courtesy, before visiting the patients, the Chaplain should approach him on the subject, and follow, so far as is possible, his suggestions as to the Chaplain's relationship to the patients. One not accustomed to visiting the sick, the unfortunate, or the imprisoned is frequently inclined to carry with him an air of gloom which he persuades himself is a manifestation of sympathy. Nobody else construes it in that light. There is no place, unless the patient be very ill, where a good joke is more highly appreciated. The sunshine of a cheerful face and the music of a genuine laugh go far toward dispelling the gloom of surroundings that are oppressive. Get in touch with the man who is sick or in the Brig by showing a genuine interest—without intruding—in his home affairs, the State from which he comes, his town; and if you happen to know anybody he knows, there will at once be a bond of mutual interest. Also provide reading matter, either from the library or some other source, for those who are unable to get in touch with such things. Offer to write letters for them and to read interesting stories or extracts from popular papers. Always see to it that no confidence that may be committed to you is betrayed.

In your visits to the Brig, while showing an interest in the inmates, be very careful to allow none of them, in his conversation, to reflect on any officer. Take "with a grain of salt" the hard luck stories and accusations with which they may regale you. Experience will teach you that in most instances men in the Brig are guilty to a greater or less degree of that with which they are charged. At the same time, when the course of wisdom permits, it is your right to do all you can to establish the innocence of the accused. In endeavoring to do this, remember that the words of the accused and the hearsay of somebody else do not constitute a proof of innocence, and officers in authority have no time to listen to what "somebody else has heard somebody else say." In other words, if it ever becomes necessary for you to appeal to authority for a man under charges, see to it that the proof which you bring really justifies you in making your appeal.

The Chaplain should visit the Brig and Sick Bay at least once a day, and oftener if he finds his visits are helpful. To fail to do this will defeat the very object of occasional visits. Very little escapes the notice of the man who has nothing to do but lie on his back and think; and if the Chaplain appears only occasionally, the first thought that comes to the patient is that surely he, the patient, must be in "bad shape" else the Chaplain would not have found it necessary to come around. The effect of such thought on a patient, of course, is not good; to avoid making such impression, the Chaplain's visits should be so frequent as to arouse no such suspicion.

When a man is desperately ill, the Chaplain should know it; and with the consent of the Senior Surgeon, should inform the patient of the fact. When a man's life is drawing to a close, opportunity should be given for such preparation, whether of spiritual or material nature, as he deems necessary. There is no greater anguish of mind than that which comes to a servant of God when he realizes that he has allowed a man to die without giving him notice of his approaching end. If the Chaplain is a Catholic and the patient a Protestant or a Jew, the Chaplain should see to it that he is attended by one of his own faith. When this order is reversed a Protestant Chaplain, when it can be possible done, should secure a rabbi or priest to minister the last rites of the church. The latter is especially important because of the emphasis which the Catholic Church places upon this Sacrament. Frequently there are convalescents on the sick list who are unable to climb the gangway to church, and an offer of the Chaplain—after consulting with the Doctor—to have someone carry them up in an easy chair will often be accepted and appreciated.

🏍 Appendix IV
Military-to-MC Chaplaincy Adaptation Table

Military Chaplaincy Reference / Standard	Military Function or Principle	Adapted Motorcycle Club Chaplain Role / Function	Practical Example in MC Context
SECNAV Instruction 1730.10A – Religious Ministry within the Department of the Navy	Defines the authority, function, confidentiality, and ethical obligation of chaplains within command structures.	The MC Chaplain serves as the club's moral and spiritual adviser, maintaining confidentiality even from leadership when necessary; authority derived from respect and trust, not rank.	When club conflict escalates, the Chaplain listens confidentially and guides reconciliation without compromising trust or political neutrality.
CHC_Chaplains_Guide_to_PNC (Professional Naval Chaplaincy)	Focuses on the "ministry of presence," resilience support, and	Emphasize "ride ministry" and clubhouse presence;	Riding in formations, visiting hospitalized members,

	mission readiness.	being where your brothers are — not preaching, but listening, being available, and walking (or riding) alongside them.	showing up at court hearings, and being a visible sign of calm and respect.
CHC Final & mPact Chaplains Handbooks	Systematic approach to counseling, worship coordinatio n, and crisis response.	Equip the MC Chaplain with tools for funerals, crisis management , addiction recovery, and moral injury healing — adapting language and tone for the biker reality.	Conducting a biker wake or memorial that honors club tradition while offering words of healing and brotherhood .
Chaplain's Guide to Professional Naval Chaplaincy (PNC Model)	Chaplains report directly to commanding officers but advocate for personnel wellbeing,	MC Chaplain reports to the president but represents the heart of the club — its moral and	Advising the president privately when internal tension or burnout

	spiritual fitness, and morale.	emotional pulse.	risk emerges in members.
The Navy Chaplain's Manual – John B. Frazier	Provides detailed guidance on religious services, ethics, confidentiality, and counseling.	A practical toolkit for structuring MC ceremonies — spiritual but not denominational; ethics remain universal: loyalty, honor, courage, respect.	Writing service outlines for patch presentations, memorial rides, and seasonal blessings of the bikes.
mPact Churches Military Chaplain Handbook	Multi-faith model: respecting all beliefs while enabling spiritual support for all.	Emphasize that the MC Chaplain serves all club members regardless of faith or lack thereof — supporting spiritual resilience rather than religious conversion.	"If he doesn't pray, you still stand by him." Respect, not religion, drives brotherhood.

Appendix V
Comprehensive Chaplain Certification Exam

Part I — Multiple Choice (75 questions)
Select the best answer (a – d).
Chapters 1–3: The Call, Origin, and Conduct

1. The word *chaplain* originates from which Latin term?
   a. Capella
   b. Cappellanus
   c. Chapaeus
   d. Capitulum
2. The story of Saint Martin of Tours centers on what symbolic act?
   a. Riding into battle without armor
   b. Sharing half his cloak with a beggar
   c. Leaving the army to become a priest
   d. Building the first roadside chapel
3. The chaplain's first duty inside a Motorcycle Club is:
   a. Preaching formal religion
   b. Managing club finances
   c. Being present and available to members
   d. Enforcing bylaws
4. Which core personal quality builds initial trust fastest?
   a. Forceful speech
   b. Steady presence
   c. Religious knowledge
   d. Rank or position
5. According to the handbook, personal discipline begins with:
   a. Spiritual study
   b. Appearance and punctuality
   c. Rapid decision making
   d. Financial contribution

6. "Above reproach" in conduct means:
   a. Avoiding friendship with members
   b. Acting beyond criticism through consistency
   c. Silently observing without engagement
   d. Quoting rules often
7. Confidentiality may be ethically broken only when:
   a. Asked by another officer
   b. Information affects life or safety
   c. Rumor control requires it
   d. Four members already know
8. The term Bridge Reflection links what two chapters?
   a. 2 → 3
   b. 3 → 4
   c. 4 → 5
   d. 6 → 7
9. "Walk the example" primarily refers to:
   a. Leading services weekly
   b. Living the code personally before teaching it
   c. Quoting scripture in meetings
   d. Fasting during major events
10. The Chaplain's Code Four lists:
    a. Teach, Lead, Pray, Correct
    b. Care, Facilitate, Provide, Advise
    c. Listen, Speak, Judge, Act
    d. Learn, Plan, Direct, Serve

Chapters 4–5: Morale & Leadership

11. Spirit, Discipline, and Code combine to form:
    a. Club Protocol
    b. Moral Backbone
    c. Operational Order
    d. Religious Policy
12. Which trait defines discipline within the Club?
    a. Strict punishment
    b. Predictable consistency

c. Blind obedience
d. Avoidance of emotion

13. The Chaplain's allegiance runs:
    a. Only to the President
    b. To Command and Conscience equally
    c. Only to fellow veterans
    d. To majority vote
14. When advising leadership, the Chaplain should:
    a. Raise objections in open meetings
    b. Provide private counsel supported by fact
    c. Speak publicly for transparency
    d. Avoid involvement altogether
15. When advising rank - and - file members, the Chaplain must:
    a. Promise outcomes
    b. Take sides in disputes
    c. Translate orders into reason
    d. Report every talk
16. Ethical neutrality means:
    a. Having no opinions
    b. Showing fairness and avoiding favoritism
    c. Supporting officers over members
    d. Voting in leadership elections
17. "Presence equals peace" means:
    a. A silent Chaplain stops fights
    b. Calm body language lowers adrenaline
    c. Physical strength secures order
    d. Religious aura commands respect
18. Upward loyalty requires the Chaplain to __________ Leadership decisions publicly.
    a. Criticize
    b. Defend
    c. Avoid
    d. Announce
19. Downward loyalty focuses on:
    a. Policy enforcement

   b. Personal care and confidentiality
   c. Club image management
   d. Spiritual lectures
20. Breaking neutrality in politics results primarily in:
   a. Promotion
   b. Loss of trust
   c. Stronger morale
   d. Faster decisions

Chapters 6–7: Care, Counsel, and Crisis

21. The two main functions of a Chaplain's daily work are:
   a. Administration and Recruiting
   b. Listening and Steadying
   c. Meditation and Finance
   d. Patrol and Security
22. "Ministry of presence" means:
   a. Preach whenever possible
   b. Be visible, available, and sincere
   c. Read lengthy devotions
   d. Lead weekly church services
23. Which practice prevents small issues from exploding?
   a. Preventive presence
   b. Formal interviews
   c. Written reprimands
   d. Group therapy
24. In crisis, first priority is always:
   a. Collecting belongings
   b. Medical / physical safety
   c. Taking photographs
   d. Calling a meeting
25. Post-incident check-ins should occur within:
   a. 24 , 48 , and 72 hours
   b. Seven days
   c. Immediately only
   d. Monthly

26. The phrase "you're not a savior; you're a steady friend" means:
    a. The Chaplain controls outcomes
    b. Presence > Preaching
    c. Referrals are failures
    d. Keep emotional distance
27. The Chaplain's field listening method begins by:
    a. Analyzing immediately
    b. Listening 2 minutes uninterrupted
    c. Offering quick advice
    d. Recording audio
28. Persistent hopelessness or suicidal talk equals:
    a. Normal frustration
    b. Immediate crisis condition
    c. Discipline issue
    d. Leadership challenge
29. Documenting care encounters in logbooks should exclude:
    a. Date
    b. Topic category
    c. Full names
    d. Follow-up plan
30. PTSD is described here as:
    a. A weakness
    b. An ongoing reaction beyond normal recovery
    c. A personality flaw
    d. A legal matter only
31. When conducting a Blessing of the Bikes, the most important tone is:
    a. Formal religion
    b. Hope and respect
    c. Humor
    d. Fear
32. A circle formation during ceremonies represents:
    a. Rank order

b. Unity and equality
c. Security perimeter
d. Speed

33. The sound of the engine rev at memorials symbolizes:
    a. Defiance
    b. Life and respect
    c. Ending
    d. Noise
34. Length of most ceremonies should be:
    a. Under 10 minutes
    b. 15–30 minutes
    c. An hour
    d. 45 minutes
35. Symbols lose power when:
    a. Explained clearly
    b. Used without meaning
    c. Personalized
    d. Repeated annually
36. When multiple clubs join a ceremony, the Chaplain should:
    a. Speak for his own club only
    b. Use neutral, unifying language
    c. Avoid protocol
    d. Skip prayer
37. Proper field documentation requires:
    a. Extensive personal data
    b. Brief factual notes
    c. Forum post
    d. None
38. Drills and exercises exist to:
    a. Fill meeting time
    b. Develop reflex under stress

c. Replace training
d. Entertain

39. The Chaplain's Toolkit purpose is:
    a. Decoration
    b. Portable readiness and reflection
    c. Tradition only
    d. Book storage
40. Phrase "Ready Body, Ready Mind, Ready Mission" comes from:
    a. Field Mindset Checklist
    b. Prospect's Bible
    c. Command Manual
    d. Ceremony Guide
41. The best time to mentor future Chaplains is:
    a. After retirement
    b. From day one of their interest
    c. Only after certification
    d. Never
42. The mentor approach emphasizes:
    a. Observation → Participation → Independence → Feedback
    b. Classroom study only
    c. Promotion interviews
    d. Annual tests only
43. Mentorship protects:
    a. Tradition and continuity
    b. Hierarchy alone
    c. Finances
    d. Confidentiality only
44. The Legacy Binder primarily stores:
    a. Financial records
    b. Ceremonies and lessons for successors

c. Visitor logs
d. Uniform regulations

45. In this handbook "legacy" means:
    a. Fame
    b. Presence beyond service
    c. Inheritance
    d. Seniority
46. The appropriate data in a Field Journal entry are:
    a. Names and addresses of members
    b. Date + topic + follow-up plan
    c. Private quotes
    d. None
47. Which phrase best defines the Chaplain's job?
    a. To enforce rules
    b. To embody the Club's conscience
    c. To replace leadership
    d. To organize finances
48. The moral impact of the Chaplain spreads mainly through:
    a. Authority
    b. Example
    c. Fear
    d. Policy
49. During an argument between officers, first action:
    a. Take sides
    b. Lower tone and restore respect
    c. Leave
    d. Quote bylaws
50. The Navy phrase "deck-plate ministry" in MC context means:
    a. Administrative chapel work
    b. Ministry in everyday spaces with hands-on presence

c. Sunday services
d. Bible study

51. Self-care for Chaplains includes:
    a. Isolation
    b. Reflection and rest
    c. Ignoring emotion
    d. Constant work
52. The most sacred contract between Chaplain and Club is:
    a. Financial trust
    b. Confidential trust
    c. Public ritual
    d. Camaraderie
53. "Proof beats preaching" refers to:
    a. 1%er leadership
    b. Corporate chaplaincy
    c. Religious conversion methods
    d. Confrontation
54. Faith in the 1%er world is usually expressed through:
    a. Dogma
    b. Loyalty and integrity shown under pressure
    c. Weekly services
    d. Written creeds
55. The Chaplain's diplomacy during legal scrutiny should be:
    a. Aggressive
    b. Calm and rational
    c. Silent and absent
    d. Defensive
56. Which is NOT a core truth about 1%er environment?
    a. Presence outweighs preaching
    b. Trust precedes listening
    c. Politics earns respect
    d. Neutrality equals survival

57. Ritual holds meaning in 1%er clubs because it:
    a. Displays authority
    b. Unites the tribe through symbol and tradition
    c. Creates religion
    d. Shows rank
58. The Rule of Three Questions safeguards:
    a. Honor and accountability
    b. Speed and obedience
    c. Profit
    d. Popularity
59. Violence response priority list begins with:
    a. Defending honor
    b. Protecting life
    c. Apportioning blame
    d. Public image
60. Legacy within the 1%er-appendix context means leaving:
    a. Money
    b. Wiser choices among brothers
    c. Written laws
    d. Promotions
61. The Blessing Card carried in the Field Kit allows:
    a. Pocket length public addresses
    b. Quick improvised reflection delivery
    c. Decorative accessory
    d. Financial tracking
62. The Quick-Draw Drill tests:
    a. Scripture memory
    b. Tone and presence under pressure
    c. Writing speed
    d. History
63. The end goal of mentorship is to:
    a. Clone skills

   b. Preserve principle over personality
   c. Replace leadership values
   d. Secure promotion
64. Recording Club memorials builds:
   a. Public relations content
   b. Continuity and honor
   c. Gossip archive
   d. Financial ledger
65. The Chaplain's calm disposition in fights serves to:
   a. Challenge authority
   b. De-escalate conflict
   c. Increase respect for force
   d. Delay action
66. When preparing a multi-faith memorial ride, the Chaplain should:

   a. Select prayers strictly from one religion only.

   b. Use inclusive language centered on loyalty and remembrance.

   c. Avoid any moment of silence.

   d. Delegate speaking duties to the loudest member.
67. If a President orders a disciplinary action that the Chaplain believes violates the Club's code, the Chaplain's first action is to:

   a. Publicly oppose the President.

   b. Privately request a meeting and present respectful counsel.

   c. Ignore the decision.

   d. Alert outside authorities immediately.
68. During a crash response when medical teams are working, the Chaplain's primary position is:

   a. Front-and-center leading a group prayer.

   b. At a respectful distance, maintaining calm and controlling crowd emotion.

c. Interviewing witnesses.

d. Filming for records.

69. Which statement defines *Service Beyond Self* as used in this handbook?

    a. Doing good deeds for public recognition.

    b. Serving brothers and Club spirit even when no credit is given.

    c. Limiting compassion to members only.

    d. Placing personal glory above duty.

70. When conducting a successor's commissioning ceremony, the outgoing Chaplain should:

    a. Deliver criticism of leadership history.

    b. Perform the oath together and transfer symbols respectfully.

    c. Leave the meeting before ceremony begins.

    d. Let officers improvise without guidance.

71. Which phrase summarizes the ethos of this Handbook?

    a. "Religious service during crisis."

    b. "Service beyond self."

    c. "Salvation through doctrine."

    d. "Power through leadership."

72. Primary symbol of unity in MC culture?

    a. MC

    b. MC patch.

    c. MC banners

    d. MC coins

73. Legacy Binder secured where – Club archive/drive.
74. Field presence teaches – Respect through example.
75. Final Reflection of book emphasizes –
    Purpose outlives position.

76. The cloak of Saint Martin later became known as the capella, giving us chapel.
77. A Chaplain's appearance has no effect on credibility.
78. Discipline protects freedom.
79. The Chaplain is always part of political voting within leadership.
80. Confidentiality only matters during funerals.
81. Moral backbone equals protocol enforcement.
82. Upward loyalty cancels downward loyalty.
83. Ride-out drills should be practiced annually.
84. PTSD can manifest months after a crash.
85. Presence ministry means being physically and emotionally available.
86. Ceremonies may be adapted for each Club as long as respect remains.
87. The Blessing of the Bikes is strictly religious and cannot be secular.
88. A Chaplain breaking neutrality loses moral authority.
89. The Field Kit should contain tokens or symbols for emergency rituals.
90. After a loss, grief follows linear stages.
91. Documentation should omit personal identifiers.
92. Mentorship means cloning the mentor exactly.
93. Succession planning begins after resignation.
94. Legacy binders are optional and discouraged.
95. A Chaplain's calm lowers group adrenaline.
96. All rituals must follow religious doctrine.
97. The Chaplain's Mentor's Table is for shared case learning.
98. Dual allegiance requires balance, not division.
99. Recording training logs improves accountability.
100. Public image is more important than ethical action.

101. A Chaplain should avoid helping members outside club eve nts.
102. Ritual language can be adapted to each club's culture.
103. Anonymous reporting destroys trust within brotherhood.
104. Professional growth requires ongoing study.
105. Laughter can be a healing act of spirit.
106. 1%er Chaplaincy rejects all structured faith principles.
107. Mentorship should begin before a crisis.
108. Military chaplaincy inspired MC discipline systems.
109. The Field Kit is optional suggestion only.
110. A good Chaplain fights every battle himself.
111. Legacy planning begins early in service.
112. Club conflict mediation is a key Chaplain duty.
113. Respect for diverse beliefs keeps clubs united.
114. Silence can be a form of ministry.
115. Documentation must include member names.
116. Presence at runs builds trust.
117. Club honor survives when discipline and compassion balance.
118. The Chaplain should model patience daily.
119. Aggression is the best response to insult.
120. Calm tone can defuse anger.
121. Succession ceremonies reinforce continuity.
122. Charity events increase community respect.
123. Legacy without mentorship fades fast.
124. Honesty and humility outweigh charisma in Chaplaincy.
125. Service ends when the ride ends.
126. Explain the historical origin of the Chaplain and apply its meaning to MC life.
127. List and define the Chaplain's Code Four.
128. Describe how personal habits influence club spirit.

129. Define "moral backbone." What three parts form it?
130. Differentiate loyalty to command from loyalty to conscience.
131. What does discipline provide that rules do not?
132. Outline the Chaplain's crash-response sequence.
133. Summarize the Seven Pillars of MC Chaplaincy.
134. Describe a Memorial Run step by step.
135. Why is neutrality critical in club politics?
136. When can confidentiality be ethically broken?
137. List three ways to practice preventive presence.
138. Explain the power of ritual for unity.
139. Define spiritual leadership in the 1%er world.
140. List three methods a Chaplain uses for self-care.
141. Write a 30-second blessing for a charity ride.
142. Explain legacy as service beyond self.
143. List three signs of a potential Chaplain candidate.
144. Describe how the Quick Reference Index improves efficiency.
145. Detail the process for correcting leadership with respect.
146. Compare military and MC chaplaincy.
147. Identify five items in the Field Kit and their meanings.
148. How should a Chaplain maintain dignity during legal scrutiny?
149. Outline how to plan your own Final Run.
150. Compose a personal creed summarizing MC Chaplain duty.

Appendix VI
Multiple Choice Answer Key

MC #	Answer	MC #	Answer	MC #	Answer
1	b	2	b	3	c
4	b	5	b	6	b
7	b	8	b	9	b
10	b	11	b	12	b
13	b	14	b	15	c
16	b	17	b	18	b
19	b	20	b	21	b
22	b	23	a	24	b
25	a	26	b	27	b
28	b	29	c	30	b
31	b	32	b	33	b
34	a	35	b	36	b
37	b	38	b	39	b
40	a	41	b	42	a
43	a	44	b	45	b
46	b	47	b	48	b
49	b	50	b	51	b
52	b	53	a	54	b
55	b	56	c	57	b
58	a	59	b	60	b
61	b	62	b	63	b
64	b	65	b	66-75	b

76. Cappa means cloak and is root of chaplain. T
77. A Chaplain's appearance affects credibility. T
78. Discipline protects freedom. T
79. Chaplain votes in leadership issues. F
80. Confidentiality matters only during funerals. F
81. Moral backbone = unwritten code of honor. T
82. Upward and downward loyalty must stay balanced. T
83. Ride-out drills are recommended annually. T
84. PTSD may appear months after trauma. T
85. Presence ministry = physical and emotional availability. T
86. Ceremonies must mirror military style exactly. F
87. Blessing of Bikes requires religious language only. F
88. Breaking neutrality costs authority. T
89. Field Kit should contain symbolic tokens. T
90. Grief moves linearly through stages. F
91. Logs omit names for privacy. T
92. Mentorship avoids cloning mentors. T
93. Succession starts before departure. T
94. Legacy binders are optional extras. F
95. Calm tone reduces adrenaline. T
96. Rituals must be unchanging forever. F
97. Mentor's Table shares lessons. T
98. Mentorship begins before crisis. T
99. Military chaplain structure inspired MC model. T
100. The Field Kit is optional suggestion. F
101. Legacy planning late is best. F
102. Chaplain de-escalates conflicts. T
103. Respect for beliefs builds unity. T
104. Silence can minister. T
105. Always publish member names in logs. F
106. Presence at rides builds trust. T
107. Balance of discipline and compassion keeps honor. T

108. Patience is optional virtue. F
109. Aggression solves insult. F
110. Calm voice defuses anger. T
111. Succession ceremonies reinforce continuity. T
112. Charity events improve public image. T
113. Legacy without mentorship vanishes. T
114. Humility beats charisma. T
115. Chaplain's service ends after death only symbolically. T
116. Being physically present at runs and events builds trust more effectively than giving long speeches. T
117. The Club maintains its honor when discipline and compassion are kept in proper balance. T
118. Patience is a core leadership habit for an MC Chaplain and should be modeled daily. T
119. Aggression is the best response when a member insults the Chaplain's authority. F
120. A Chaplain's calm voice can defuse anger and reduce emotional escalation during conflicts. T
121. Conducting a formal succession ceremony helps reinforce continuity and respect when a new Chaplain takes office. T
122. Participating in charity events and community outreach enhances the motorcycle club's public reputation. T
123. Without mentorship, a Chaplain's legacy usually fades and is not carried into the next generation. T
124. Honesty and humility are more important than charisma for long-term credibility in Chaplaincy. T
125. A Chaplain's service ends the moment he stops riding or holds no formal title. F (Reason: A Chaplain's influence — like leadership — endures long after the role changes.)
126. **Explain the historical origin of the Chaplain and apply its meaning to MC life:** The word *chaplain* comes from the Latin *cappellanus*, keeper of Saint Martin's half-cloak. Martin cut his soldier's cloak to warm a freezing beggar, symbolizing courage and compassion. In MC life, the

Chaplain follows the same example: share strength, offer comfort, and serve brothers without judgment.

127. **List and define the Chaplain's Code Four:** Care (support every member), Facilitate (ensure unity & morale), Provide (guidance or rituals when asked), Advise (offer ethical counsel to leadership).
128. **Describe how personal habits influence club spirit:** A Chaplain's discipline sets the tone: showing up early, speaking calmly, keeping confidence, and being emotionally steady. Members mirror this energy, shaping the club's morale.
129. **Define "moral backbone." What three parts form it:** Moral backbone is the invisible structure that keeps a club honorable. It's made of Spirit (morale), Discipline (order), and Code (values).
130. **Differentiate loyalty to command from loyalty to conscience:** Loyalty to command means supporting leadership decisions publicly. Loyalty to conscience means speaking truth privately when decisions threaten ethics or unity. A Chaplain balances both.
131. **What does discipline provide that rules do not:** Rules control behavior, but discipline shapes character. Discipline keeps freedom functional and prevents chaos during conflict.
132. **Outline the Chaplain's crash-response sequence:** Ensure safety, maintain calm presence, reassure injured person, manage crowd emotion, support medics without interfering, notify leadership, follow up with affected members in 24/48/72 hours.
133. **Summarize the Seven Pillars of MC Chaplaincy:** Presence, Confidentiality, Counsel, Ceremony Leadership, Crisis Response, Ethical Advisory, and Mentorship/Legacy.

134. **Describe a Memorial Run step by step:** Plan route, organize safety, coordinate with family, open with reflection, read names, conduct moment of silence or engine salute, ride in formation, conclude with words of unity and remembrance.
135. **Why is neutrality critical in club politics:** It ensures trust. If a Chaplain takes sides, he loses credibility with the entire club and can no longer mediate conflict or advise leadership.
136. **When can confidentiality be ethically broken:** Only when a life is at risk or a threat endangers the club's safety. Otherwise, confidentiality is absolute.
137. **List three ways to practice preventive presence:** Attend runs, check in on members regularly, visit hospitals or homes, show up early at meetings, join wrench nights. (Any three.)
138. **Explain the power of ritual for unity:** Rituals create shared meaning, reinforce identity, honor history, and connect members emotionally. They turn events into traditions and strengthen cohesion.
139. **Define spiritual leadership in the 1%er world:** It's not preaching — it's demonstrating loyalty, courage, discretion, and emotional steadiness. A 1%er Chaplain leads by presence, not doctrine.
140. **List three methods a Chaplain uses for self-care:** Solo rides, reflection/prayer, talking with another Chaplain, physical fitness, time with family, journaling, rest. (Any three.)
141. **Write a 30-second blessing for a charity ride:** "May these miles bring hope to those who need it most. Let our hearts stay humble, our wheels stay steady, and our purpose stay

pure. Ride safe, ride true, and ride for something bigger than ourselves."

142. **Explain legacy as service beyond self:** Legacy means influencing the club long after the Chaplain steps down — through habits, rituals, and culture he helped shape. It's the echo of his example.
143. **List three signs of a potential Chaplain candidate:** Respect from all ranks, calm temperament, trustworthy with secrets, consistent presence, emotional intelligence. (Any three.)
144. **Describe how the Quick Reference Index improves efficiency.** It gives instant access to crisis steps, ceremonies, tools, and drills without flipping through full chapters. In emergencies, seconds matter.
145. **Detail the process for correcting leadership with respect:** Request private meeting, state facts calmly, frame concerns around club code, offer options, accept final decision, maintain unity publicly.
146. **Compare military and MC chaplaincy:** Both serve diverse members, keep confidence, advise leaders, stabilize morale, and lead rituals. MC chaplaincy mirrors "ministry of presence" from military but adapts for biker culture.
147. **Identify five items in the Field Kit and their meanings:** Notebook (memory & guidance), coin/patch (symbol of unity), candle/light (reflection), multi-tool (readiness), handkerchief (comfort), blessing card (ritual support), emergency contacts (care). Any five with meaning.
148. **How should a Chaplain maintain dignity during legal scrutiny:** Stay calm, speak factually, avoid club politics, avoid inflammatory comments, coordinate with leadership, never speak without authorization, project respectfulness.

149. **Outline how to plan your own Final Run:** Choose route, designate who carries colors or ashes, select readings or final words, coordinate with family, request Chaplain successor's involvement, define symbolic elements (rev salute, patch presentation).
150. **Compose a personal creed summarizing MC Chaplain duty:** Sample answer: "I serve with humility, protect trust, calm storms, honor the fallen, and care for every brother. My presence is my sermon, and my loyalty is my oath."

SCORING RUBRIC

Section	Questions	Points Each	Possible Points
Multiple Choice	75	1	75
True / False	50	1	50
Essay	25	2	50
Total			175

Performance Levels
- Outstanding 165-175 (94-100 %)
- Proficient 140-164 (80-93 %)
- Needs Development < 140

EVALUATOR CERTIFICATION

Evaluator Name ____
Signature ____
Date ________________
Result ☐ PASS ☐ PROVISIONAL ☐ RETEST

Archival Instructions

- Attach graded answer sheet to candidate record.
- Enter results into Chapter Training Binder / Regional Roster.
- Destroy any scrap notes to preserve confidentiality.

"A test doesn't create a Chaplain — it confirms the quiet giants who already are."
— Black Dragon

End of Certification Packet

⚔ Appendix VII
A Brief History of U.S. Army Chaplaincy

1 – Birth of the Chaplaincy (1775 – 1789)

- On **July 29, 1775**—just a day after Congress created the Continental Army—it authorized **one chaplain for each regiment.**
  That date marks the birth of the U. S. Army Chaplain Corps.
- Early chaplains were volunteer clergy who received pay equal to that of a captain and were expected to preach, pray, write letters for illiterate soldiers, and keep morale high on the march.
- The first recorded Army chaplains included **Reverend Abiel Leonard** and **Reverend John Hurt**, serving under General George Washington, himself a man who demanded daily prayers and Sabbath observance in camp.

Washington's view: "A moral and religious Army is the surest means of preserving liberty." He insisted that chaplains nurture both discipline and conscience — exactly what I advocate inside motorcycle clubs.

2 – Early Republic through Civil War (1790 – 1865)

- After the Revolution, the chaplaincy survived even as the Army shrank.
- Chaplains in frontier forts often doubled as schoolteachers, moral stewards, and community pastors for settlers.
- The War of 1812 and Mexican-American War expanded responsibilities: burying the dead, conducting worship under fire, and comforting prisoners.
- In 1838 Congress formalized the **Chaplain Corps** as a permanent part of the Army and authorized **commissioned officer** status.

- During the **Civil War**, over 2,000 chaplains served both Union and Confederate forces.
    - Dozens were captured in battle while tending wounded from both sides.
    - The first **Black Army chaplain, Rev. Henry McNeal Turner**, was appointed in 1863 to minister to the U.S. Colored Troops—an early step toward a diverse corps.

3 – Reconstruction to World War I (1866 – 1917)

- Post-war chaplains in frontier outposts served small garrisons, Native American missions, and early ROTC schools.
- The 1898 Spanish-American War introduced **chaplains aboard troop transports**, creating the bridge to the Navy's later joint work and setting precedents for field burial rites and combat stress care.
- By 1917, systematic chaplain training began at **Camp Zachary Taylor, Kentucky**, forming the genesis of the **U.S. Army Chaplain School.**

4 – World Wars and "The Four Chaplains" (1918 – 1945)

- In WW I and WW II, chaplains proved indispensable for morale and ethics.
- Over **9,000 Army chaplains** served in WWII; 142 were killed in action; eleven received the Distinguished Service Cross.
- The most famous episode: **February 3, 1943 — The Four Chaplains** (a Methodist, a Jewish Rabbi, a Catholic Priest, and a Reformed minister) sacrificed their lifejackets and prayed together as the troopship *Dorchester* sank in the North Atlantic. Their unity under fire became the emblem of pluralism and "faith in action."

5 – Korea, Vietnam, and the Cold War (1950 – 1990)

- Korea's front lines introduced mobile chapels and helicopter extraction of wounded under chaplain care.
- Vietnam expanded the corps' counseling, suicide-prevention, and moral-advisement roles.
- In 1974, the Chaplain School moved to **Fort Jackson, South Carolina**, where it remains as the **U.S. Army Institute for Religious Leadership.**
- Diversity broadened: Protestant, Catholic, Jewish, Orthodox, Buddhist, Muslim, and other credentialed clergy began to serve side by side.

6 – Modern Era and Global Operations (1990 – Present)

- Desert Storm, Iraq, and Afghanistan solidified chaplains as integral staff officers.
- Their mandate: **"Nurture the Living, Care for the Wounded, and Honor the Fallen."**
- Today roughly **1,200 active-duty chaplains** serve alongside **600 religious-affairs specialists** worldwide, covering more than **200 denominations and faith groups.**
- Training emphasizes cross-cultural competence, crisis-intervention, ethical advisement, and resilient-leader coaching — skills mirrored almost exactly in this MC chaplain model.

7 – Core Army Chaplain Values

Value	Practical Translation
Presence	Go where soldiers (or riders) are — not wait for them to come to you.
Pluralism	Serve everyone's conscience, not just your own creed.
Confidentiality	Sacred trust — the conversation never leaves the tent (or clubhouse).
Courage under Fire	Remain when others run; calm is contagious.
Service Beyond Self	The heart of chaplaincy in any uniform.

8 – Legacy
Since 1775, the Army Chaplain Corps has served in every major U.S. conflict, often unarmed and under fire, proving that **moral strength sustains physical courage.**
Their motto, **"Pro Deo et Patria" (For God and Country)**, parallels biker culture: *For Brotherhood and Honor.*
Relevance to MC Chaplains

- Both institutions demand loyalty, composure, and belief in something greater than themselves.
- Both operate in tight communities where trust is currency.
- And both rely on individuals who keep the spiritual engine running when others only see the metal and noise.

From holy ground to muddy trenches to the open highway, the Chaplain's mission has never changed:
be there, and keep the flame lit.

⚓ Appendix VII
A Brief History of U.S. Naval Chaplaincy

1 – Colonial Origins (1775 – 1794)

- **July 28, 1775** – The Continental Congress voted to provide a chaplain on every ship of the Continental Navy. This predates even the Declaration of Independence, showing that *moral and spiritual care* were viewed as critical to naval readiness from the start.
- The earliest known chaplain, **Reverend Benjamin Balch**, served aboard the USS Boston during the Revolution, leading prayers, counseling sailors, and maintaining morale at sea.

When the Navy disbanded after the Revolution, chaplaincy followed it into dormancy until the fleet was re-established.

2 – Formal Establishment (1794 – 1860)

- **1794:** Congress authorized construction of six frigates and directed that each carry a commissioned chaplain.
- Early responsibilities blended religious services with instruction, moral oversight, and even postal duties for the crew.
- Chaplains were civilians until **1862**, when Congress granted them commissioned-officer status, recognizing their leadership importance.

These early chaplains were almost exclusively Protestant clergy; pluralism developed slowly as America's faith landscape broadened.

3 – Civil War to World War I (1861 – 1918)

- Civil War chaplains served with both the Navy and the Marine Corps, often crossing enemy lines to minister to prisoners and the wounded.
- **1878:** The Bureau of Navigation (forerunner of the Navy Personnel Command) created the **Chaplain Corps** as a distinct entity.
- Duties expanded to instruction in literacy and ethics, prevention of vice in port cities, and support for sailors far from home.
- By World War I, the Corps had formal training standards under guidance from senior chaplain **William F. Cassard**.

4 – Interwar & World War II (1919 – 1945)

- Interwar decades professionalized chaplaincy further—doctrinally neutral, focused on morale and welfare.
- During WWII, chaplains deployed on every ship, base, and battlefield—from Tarawa to Okinawa.
- Over **2,900 Navy chaplains** served between 1941-45; many earned valor awards, and sixteen made the ultimate sacrifice.
- This period birthed the **"ministry of presence"** doctrine: a chaplain's power was not in preaching but in *being there* in the worst moments.

5 – Cold War Era (1946 – 1990)

- Chaplains accompanied fleets to Korea, Vietnam, and the nuclear submarine force I once called home.
- Submarine and aviation chaplaincies demanded exceptional confidentiality and resilience — precisely the character traits I describe for MC life.
- The Corps embraced diversity, commissioning Jewish, Catholic, and later Muslim and Orthodox chaplains, reflecting the pluralism of the modern Navy.

- Doctrinal focus shifted toward **pastoral care, ethics consultation, and family support.**

6 – Modern Era (1990 – Present)

- Post-9/11 operations in Iraq, Afghanistan, and humanitarian missions worldwide widened the chaplain's field role: trauma counseling, moral advisement on rules of engagement, suicide prevention, leadership mentoring.
- The official guiding directive became **SECNAV Instruction 1730.10 series (1997 – present)**, defining the chaplain's four core capabilities:
  1. Provide religious ministry.
  2. Facilitate free exercise for all service members.
  3. Care for all regardless of faith.
  4. Advise commanders on morale, ethics, and spirituality.

Today's Navy Chaplain Corps—headquartered in Arlington, VA—consists of roughly **600 active-duty chaplains** and **200 Reserve chaplains**, serving alongside Religious Program Specialists in more than 40 faith traditions.

7 – Traditions Worth Translating to the MC World

Navy Tradition	Translated MC Application
***Ministry of Presence* – be physically among the crew**	Ride among your brothers, not above them.
***Pluralism* – care for all faiths and none**	Serve every patch equally, spiritual or secular.
Confidential Counsel	Keep clubhouse trust tighter than chain oil.
***Ethical Advisement* – counsel Command on morale**	Whisper wisdom to leadership, never gossip.
***Pastoral Care under Fire* – stability amid danger**	Stay calm at accidents, funerals, and conflicts.

8 – Legacy Motto

"Called to Serve – Ready to Stand – Committed to Care."

That Navy Chaplain Corps motto captures precisely the identity of the motorcycle-club chaplain: **a presence of calm, courage, and compassion inside a warrior culture**.

⚓ Appendix IX
A Brief History of Naval Chaplaincy Serving the Marine Corps

1 – Shared Roots (1775 – 1860)

- Both the **U.S. Navy** and the **U.S. Marine Corps** were established in **1775** under the Continental Congress.
- Because Marines originated as **naval infantry**—troops who served aboard ships and protected sailors—the spiritual support for those Marines naturally came from the same chaplain ministering to the ship's crew.
- The first documented Marine worship services were led by shipboard Navy chaplains in the late 1770s. There was no need, or manpower, for a separate corps.

2 – Formal Arrangement (1860s – 1918)

- When Congress officially recognized the **U.S. Navy Chaplain Corps** in 1862, that corps became responsible for providing chaplains to all departments under the Secretary of the Navy—including the Marine Corps.
- The relationship was simple: **Marines fight; Navy supports — on sea and shore alike.**
- By the Spanish-American War, Marine Corps expeditionary forces such as those in Cuba, Haiti, and the Philippines always deployed with a Navy chaplain attached for moral and religious care.

3 – World War I & II — The Bond Deepens

- In WW I, Navy chaplains accompanied Marines in France's trenches, notably at Belleau Wood (1918).

  - Chaplains conducted field burials, wrote letters home for the fallen, and coordinated Red Cross family care.
- During WW II, the partnership became legendary.
  - Every Marine division, regiment, and ship detachment had Navy chaplains present—on Guadalcanal, Iwo Jima, Okinawa, and hundreds of smaller engagements.
  - Navy Chaplains like **Lt. George Fox**, one of the Four Chaplains, and **Lt. Father Vincent Capodanno**, the "Grunt Chaplain," became icons of courage among Marines.
  - Capodanno was posthumously awarded the **Medal of Honor** for ministering to wounded Marines under fire in Vietnam (1967).

4 – Postwar to Present (1950s – Today)

- The practice of **dual service** continues: Navy chaplains are permanently assigned to Marine Corps units, schools, air stations, and expeditionary forces.
- Chaplains wear the **Navy insignia** and uniform but operate as fully integrated members of the Marine command structure, advising commanders on morale and ethics exactly as if they were Marines themselves.
- The Corps' spiritual motto is borrowed proudly from its Navy partners:
  "Provide, Facilitate, Care, Advise."

Current structure:

MARINE UNIT TYPE	CHAPLAIN COVERAGE
MARINE EXPEDITIONARY FORCE (MEF)	Senior Navy Chaplain + staff of 4–8
REGIMENTS /BATTALIONS / WINGS	One Navy Chaplain each
MARINE CORPS RECRUIT DEPOTS (PARRIS ISLAND, SAN DIEGO)	Multi-faith chapel teams of Navy Chaplains and Religious Program Specialists

5 – Symbols and Shared Identity

- Navy chaplains assigned to Marines traditionally wear the **Marine Corps service uniform** with Navy rank and insignia.
- Marines affectionately call them **"Padres"**, **"Sky Pilots,"** or **"Gunfighter Chaplains."**
- They train at the same physical-fitness standards, attend field exercises, live in combat outposts, and, in every sense but title, *become* Marines.
- The Navy's Religious Program Specialists (RPs) often train alongside Marines as well, performing security and logistics for the chaplain—another unique partnership since chaplains themselves remain non-combatants.

6 – Modern Chaplains in Combat and Counsel

From Iraq and Afghanistan to humanitarian operations, Navy chaplains assigned to Marine commands have:

- Led memorials on flight decks and in dusty forward-operating-bases.
- Delivered stress-control and suicide-prevention programs.
- Served as ethical advisors to commanders.
- Provided cross-faith worship, including for non-religious troops seeking guidance.

Their watchword remains **"Called to Serve — Ready to Stand."**

7 – Why It Matters to this Handbook

The Marine-Navy model you see here is exactly the framework the *MC Chaplain* program mirrors:

NAVY CHAPLAIN	MARINE UNIT SERVED	MC PARALLEL
SPIRITUAL COUNSEL WITHOUT COMMAND AUTHORITY	Combat-ready unit	Chaplain in 1% world—moral support without leadership rank
PRESENCE WITH FIGHTERS UNDER STRESS	Battlefield	Clubhouse or run under pressure
DRESS THE SAME, SHARE THE RISK BUT CARRY NO WEAPON	Warfighter cult ure with consci ence	Biker culture with brotherhood
REPORTS THROUGH NAVY C OMMAND BUT SERVES MA RINES DIRECTLY	Dual loyalty	Dual allegiance (Leadership & Co nscience)

Their relationship proves that **spiritual leadership doesn't require its own corps — just courage and cooperation.**

"Wherever Marines go, their Padres go too — unarmed, unafraid, and never unneeded."

Summary

- **Founded:** 1775 (service provided by Navy chaplains)
- **Independence:** None – under Department of the Navy
- **Motto:** *Called to Serve – Ready to Stand*
- **Size:** ~250 Navy Chaplains assigned yearly across Marine units
- **Distinctive Mark:** Combat-tested ministry of presence directly integrated into front-line commands.

So, while the **Marines don't commission their own chaplains**, their relationship with the **Navy Chaplain Corps** remains one of the tightest service partnerships in the U.S. military—a model any MC Chaplain can learn from: unity of mission, shared danger, and unshakable loyalty between warrior and shepherd.

Appendix X
A Brief History of the U.S. Air Force Chaplaincy

1 – Origins Before the Air Force (1917 – 1946)

For its first three decades, military aviation fell under the U.S. Army. When the **Army Air Corps** took shape during World War I, chaplains already serving soldiers simply expanded their work to flying units. They preached in hangars, counseled crews who were confronting a completely new kind of combat, and comforted families after missions gone wrong.

By World War II the **Army Air Forces** operated almost as an independent service, with over **2,000 chaplains** spread across bomber groups, fighter squadrons, and air bases worldwide. One of them, **Chaplain Earl B. Hanson**, flew multiple combat missions so he could minister on return. Their focus became "morale in the air and meaning on the ground."

2 – Birth of the U.S. Air Force Chaplain Corps (1947 – 1950)

- **September 18, 1947:** The National Security Act created the **United States Air Force** as a separate branch.
- Within weeks the new service organized its own **Chaplain Corps**, splitting formally from the Army's.
- **Major General Charles I. Carpenter, USAF**, a WWII veteran chaplain, became the first **Chief of Chaplains**.

Founding Principles (1949 Directive AFR 265-1):

1. Provide ministry to all Air Force personnel and families.
2. Ensure free exercise of religion for every Airman.
3. Advise commanders on morale, ethics, and welfare.
4. Develop pastoral programs suited to a global, high-technology force.

3 – Cold War Years (1950 – 1991)

The jet age gave chaplaincy a completely new environment: missile silos, nuclear bombers, remote radar sites, and bases from Alaska to Guam. Chaplains were often the only non-technical officers free to visit every area and talk about *why* people served, not just *how.*

Key milestones:

- **1950 – Korean War:** Chaplains rotated to forward airfields, sometimes within artillery range, ministering to pilots who flew multiple dangerous sorties each day.
- **1960s – Space Age & Vietnam:** Air Force chaplains opened field centers at major hospitals and forward operating bases in Thailand and Vietnam.
    - Several earned Silver and Bronze Star medals.
    - Emphasis grew on counseling and family support as tours lengthened.
- **1971:** The Chaplain School moved to **Maxwell Air Force Base, Alabama**, later named the **Chaplain Corps College**.
- Diversity expanded steadily: Catholic, Protestant, Jewish, and Eastern Orthodox clergy joined, followed later by Islamic, Buddhist, and other endorsing faiths.

The Cold War defined the motto still used today: **"Glorifying God, Strengthening Airmen, Serving All."**

4 – Modern Operations (1991 – Present)

After the Gulf War, chaplain responsibilities multiplied—spanning combat stress, humanitarian missions, and 24-hour global deployments.

- **1990s:** In Bosnia, Kosovo, and Desert Storm, chaplains handled multi-faith worship in joint environments and established trauma-care teams with mental-health professionals.

- **Post-9/11:** The Air Force Chaplain Corps deployed in Operations Enduring Freedom and Iraqi Freedom, often embedding with forward Air Support Operations Groups.
- **21st-Century Chaplaincy:**
    - Provides counseling on ethics of remote warfare (drone operations).
    - Serves psychological-resilience programs like *Airman Family Readiness and Spiritual Fitness.*
    - Works closely with Religious Affairs Airmen (formerly Chaplain Assistants) for logistics and data-privacy control.

Today the Corps consists of roughly **500 active-duty chaplains, 300 Reserve and Guard chaplains**, and **900 Religious Affairs Airmen** supporting more than **600,000 total-force Airmen and dependents** worldwide.

5 – Distinctive Features of Air Force Chaplaincy

Feature	Description / Application
Technology & Mobility	Chaplains travel globally at a moment's notice — parallels MC runs spanning regions or countries.
Integration with Command	Advisory role on unit morale & decision ethics mirrors Chaplain advisory function to MC presidency.
Wingman Culture	Emphasizes every member's duty to watch each other's six — the same "no one rides alone" ethic of club life.
Interfaith Ministry	Chaplains work across hundreds of belief systems — skills essential for diverse MC membership.
Family Support	Focus on spouse programs parallels attention this book urges the MC Chaplain to give club families.

6 – Mottos and Mission Statements

- **Motto:** *"We Serve God and Man."*
- **Vision Statement (Modern):** "To inspire readiness of the Spirit while caring for Airmen and families anytime, anywhere."
- **Core Capabilities:** Provide • Advise • Care • Connect.

7 – Legacy and Influence

For three-quarters of a century, Air Force chaplains have stood at flight lines, missile alert facilities, hospitals, and deployed tents reminding Airmen that courage and conscience must fly in formation.

Their professionalism shaped joint-service doctrine and modern pastoral-care models used across the Armed Forces—and, by extension, any tight community under stress. The same DNA appears in the MC Chaplain's Handbook: competence under pressure, quiet presence, and loyalty seasoned with empathy.

Whether in a cockpit at 30,000 feet or on a Harley in the rain, the Chaplain's job is identical — keep the human soul from stalling out.

⚓ Appendix XI
A Brief History of U.S. Coast Guard Chaplaincy

1 – Early Beginnings (1790 – 1915)

- The Coast Guard traces its roots to the **U.S. Revenue Marine**, established on **August 4, 1790**, to enforce customs laws on the new nation's waters.
- During these early years, the cutters were small—typically fewer than 20 men—and had **no commissioned chaplains.** Moral and spiritual care fell to the ship's captain or to local port clergy.
- As the service developed through the 19th century, it remained a seagoing law-enforcement and rescue organization, not yet large enough to field an official clergy corps.

2 – Toward Formal Support (1915 – World War II)

- In **1915**, the Revenue Cutter Service and the **U.S. Life-Saving Service** merged to form the modern **United States Coast Guard (USCG)**, under the Treasury Department.
- Still, its ships and bases were too small or dispersed for a dedicated clergy roster. Chaplains from nearby communities or the Navy often visited when possible.
- The need for spiritual and moral support became clearer as missions expanded—law enforcement, immigration patrols, and rescue.

3 – World War II: The First Coast Guard Chaplains

- With war approaching, President Roosevelt ordered the Coast Guard transferred to the **Navy Department (1941 – 1946).**

- For the first time, **Navy Chaplains** were formally assigned to Coast Guard ships and stations.
  They conducted services aboard troop transports, cutters, and beach-head operations—including **D-Day landings** and Pacific invasions under Coast Guard control.
- The first official **Chief of Chaplains (acting)** for the CG element was **Lt Cdr Daniel A. Poling**, a Reserve chaplain later famous among "The Four Chaplains."
- Over 80 Navy Chaplains served with the Coast Guard in WWII, ministering to more than 250,000 personnel.

4 – Peace and Expansion (1946 – 1970s)

- After the war, the Coast Guard returned to the Treasury Department (and later the Department of Transportation in 1967), but the agreement with the **U.S. Navy Chaplain Corps** continued:
  No separate CG corps would be created; all clergy support would come from Navy chaplains on extended assignment.
- In 1952 the Commandant issued the first **policy letter codifying chaplain duties**, making them part of the Commandant's Religious Ministries Program.
- Chaplains served at key training centers—Cape May (NJ), Alameda (CA), and Yorktown (VA)—and aboard high-endurance cutters on long ocean patrols.

5 – Modern Era (1980 – Present)
Organizational Structure

- Although still administratively under the Navy Chaplain Corps, the CG operates its own **Chaplain of the Coast Guard** office within the Commandant's staff at Headquarters (Washington D.C.).
- The position is held by a senior Navy Chaplain (O-6 Captain) who also serves as Deputy Chief of Navy Chaplains for Coast Guard Matters.

Mission

"To facilitate the free exercise of religion for Coast Guard personnel and families, enhance morale, and promote ethical decision-making throughout the service."

Numbers

- Roughly **45 – 50 active-duty Navy Chaplains** serve Coast Guard units at any given time, assisted by Reserve Chaplains and local volunteer clergy.
- They operate across 15 districts, serving 40,000 active-duty members and 8,000 reservists.

Key Deployments & Roles

- Domestic disaster relief (Hurricane Katrina, Hurricanes Sandy and Harvey).
- Overseas security operations (Operation Iraqi Freedom port missions).
- Search-and-rescue command centers, cutters, air wings, and training commands.
- Counseling on stress, grief, suicide prevention, and family separation.

6 – Distinctive Values of Coast Guard Chaplains

CORE VALUE	MEANING IN SERVICE	PARALLEL FOR MC CHAPLAINS
SEMPER PARATUS (ALWAYS READY)	Constant readiness to deploy with their crews at sea or ashore.	Be ready 24/7 for club crises and runs.
SMALL-UNIT MINISTRY	One chaplain may serve hundreds across multiple bases —	One Chaplain often covers several chapters.

	adaptability is key.	
INTER-AGENCY COOPERATION	Works with Homeland Security, FEMA, local clergy.	Cooperate with outside clubs and civil groups.
HUMANITARIAN CRISIS SUPPORT	Chaplains assist rescue crews during disasters.	Provide aid and moral support during community tragedies.
PROFESSIONAL NEUTRALITY	Serve all personnel regardless of belief or duty type.	Serve every patch and faith without bias.

7 – Leadership Lineage

Era	Notable Chaplains / Events
WW II	LCDR Daniel A. Poling – among the Four Chaplains of the *Dorchester* (1943)
1960s-70s	Chaplains supported Vietnam-era port security detachments
1990s	Chaplain Gordon R. O'Brien became first formal "Chaplain of the Coast Guard"
2000s – Now	Chaplains regularly deploy to disaster zones and joint combatant commands with Navy and Marine counterparts

8 – Philosophy and Motto

"Called to Serve — Always Ready to Stand."

The motto combines Navy Chaplaincy's call to service with the Coast Guard's operational credo, *Semper Paratus.*

It defines what your MC Chaplains strive for: faith practiced in motion, not behind a podium.

9 – Legacy
For more than 80 years of formal partnership, **Navy Chaplains assigned to the Coast Guard have fulfilled a unique dual identity**:

- Fully Navy in uniform and commissioning.
- Entirely Coast Guard in mission and mindset.

They embody what you preach to MC Chaplains—*blend in without losing who you are.*

They prove that loyalty, adaptability, and courage can coexist with compassion.
"Whether rescuing souls from stormy seas or from storms within, a Chaplain's task remains the same — keep hope afloat."

Summary Table

Founded / Authorized	**Primary Authority**	**Parent Corps**	**Approx. Chaplains**	**Motto**
WW II (1942 officially)	Commandant, U.S. Coast Guard	U.S. Navy Chaplain Corps	45–50 Active / 20 Reserve	*Semper Paratus – Always Ready to Serve*

Connection to MC Chaplaincy
Just like Navy-to-Marine integration, the Coast Guard model illustrates:

- A small, distributed organization maintaining *big-service* values through partnership.
- Chaplains who operate autonomously at distant posts, much like independent club chapters.
- A culture of **readiness, adaptability, and compassion without compromise**—ideals every MC Chaplain can emulate.

⚓ About the Author

John E. Bunch II 'Black Dragon' rode on the back of a Honda Trail 50cc for the first time when he was six years old. Instantly, he was hooked! His mother could not afford to buy him a motorcycle so he borrowed anyone's bike that would let him ride- on the back roads and farms all over Oklahoma where he grew up. When he was fourteen his mother bought him a Yamaha 125 Enduro, cashing in the US Savings Bonds his father had given him. By the time he was seventeen, his stepfather, J.W. Oliver, gave him a Honda CX500. He was known throughout the neighborhood as the kid who always rode wheelies up the block (16th street and Classen), and as the kid who always rode wheelies with his brothers, Thea, and Lori, hanging off the back. He took his first long distance road trip at seventeen riding from Oklahoma City to Wichita, Kansas to visit his aunt and uncle. He knew then that he was born to distance ride! The nomadic call of the open road in the wind, rain, cold, heat—under the stars were home to him.

In the late 1980s, he found himself a young submarine sailor stationed in San Diego, California. He got into trouble on the base with a Senior Chief who gave him and his best friend an order they refused to follow. The white Senior Chief did not want to see the young Black man's career ended over insubordination, so he did Bunch an extreme favor. He sent him and his insolent friend, Keith (Alcatraz) Corley, who was similarly in trouble; to see African American, then Senior Chief, George G. Clark III, instead of to a Courts Martial. Senior Chief Clark threatened Bunch and Corley with physical violence if they did not obey the white Senior Chief and worked out a solution that saved both of their careers. Later, Clark invited them to 4280 Market Street when he discovered Bunch had a love for motorcycles. Bunch walked into the mother chapter and was blown away to learn that Senior Chief Clark was also known as 'Magic', former President of the Black Sabbath Motorcycle Club Mother Chapter. His insubordinate ways were not quite behind him, so it took Bunch several years to actually cross over as a full patch brother known as 'Black Dragon' in the Black Sabbath Motorcycle Club Mother Chapter.

In 2000, Black Dragon began advising writer/filmmaker Reggie Rock Bythewood, who co-wrote and directed the Dream Works movie Biker Boyz. Black Dragon went to Hollywood and worked as the Technical Adviser on the film. Biker Boyz has often been credited with re-birthing the African American MC movement in the United States.

In 2000 Black Dragon brought the Black Sabbath Motorcycle Club to Atlanta, GA and was blessed by President Skull of the Outcast MC Nation to start the chapter but the Atlanta chapter never really gained steam until he got serious about it in 2009. He suffered his first setback in Atlanta during a coup d'état that cost him the Presidency of the Atlanta chapter in December 2010. In February 2011, he was elected to the Office of National President and began his nationwide march to spread the Black Sabbath Motorcycle Club from coast to coast. By 2011, the Black Sabbath Motorcycle Club became the Mighty Black Sabbath Motorcycle Club Nation with chapters from the West coast to the East coast.

2002 to 2013 Black Dragon has published several biker magazines including: *Urban Biker Cycle News, Black Iron Motorcycle Magazine, Black Sabbath Motorcycle Newsletter,* and the popular blog *www.blacksabbathmagazine.com.*

In 2013, Black Dragon wrote his first MC phone app, *"Black Sabbath Motorcycle Club."*

In 2014 Black Dragon wrote *"Prospect's Bible"* which has become required reading for over 3,000 MCs worldwide. It was his first book in the Motorcycle Club Bible series.

In 2015 Black Dragon wrote *"MC Public Relations Officer's Bible"* and *"Prospect's Bible for Women's MCs"* the second and third books in the Motorcycle Club Bible series.

In 2016 Black Dragon started the wildly popular YouTube channel "Black Dragon National President" which eventually became "Black Dragon Biker TV." It quickly rose to become the number 1 MC protocol and biker news channel in the country. He also created the online news magazine www.bikerliberty.com.

In 2017 Black Dragon wrote *"Sergeant at Arms Bible"* the fourth book in the Motorcycle Club Bible series, and was the keynote speaker at the MC Professional Convention (PROC) one of the largest MC education conferences in the United States.

In 2018 Black Dragon was again invited to speak at the PROC.

In 2019 Black Dragon created the podcast "The Dragon's Lair Motorcycle Chaos" on the Spreaker podcasting platform.

In 2020, during the height of the pandemic, Black Dragon became the first African American to be awarded the Silver Spoke Award "for improving the image of biking in the category of media and entertainment" from the National Coalition of Motorcyclist. This coveted award he shares with Charleston Heston, Jay Leno, "Hollywood" James Masecari, Big Bone 1%er OFFO and Howie of Final Option MC.

In 2021 Black Dragon wrote the best seller "President's Bible Chronicle I, Principles of Motorcycle Club Leadership" the fifth book in the Motorcycle Club Bible series.

In 2023 Black Dragon launched "BlackDragonBikerTV" TikTok and went to 93 thousand subscribers in eight months.

In 2023 November 6th Black Dragon was honored to be invited to participate in the rap 1% unification song … by Taa Shon 1%er (Thunderguards MC) and Pipeline 1%er (Outcast MC). This rap song announced a truce between all major 1% Black and mixed-race OMC nations operating on the Black biker set. Black Dragon had a cameo appearance in the music video which can be found at https://www.youtube.com/watch?v=4eZBEUbLar0. In this video members from Outcast MC, Thunderguards MC, Chosen Few MC, and Wheels of Soul MC can be seen.

In 2023 Black Dragon was honored to be included on the El Domino song "Diamond on my Heart (Outlaw Biker Anthem) featuring Big Buzz and Black Dragon on the El Domino comeback album, "The Preacher The Gangster The Outlaw" featuring Snoop Dogg, Three 6 Mafia, Akon, T-Pain, The Game, Baby Bash and Mr. Criminal. The music video "Diamond on my Heart" was produced by three-time Emmy award winning director Joshua Coombs. Black Dragon did the voiceover in the music video quoting former South African President Nelson Mandella, *"A wise man once said, when a man is denied the right to live the life he believes in, he has no choice but to become an outlaw."*

On December 10, 2023, Black Dragon published *"Social Clubs Bible Revival of the Black Women's Social Clubs Movement Lifting as We Climb!"* This was his sixth book in the Motorcycle Club Bible series.

In November of 2024, Black Dragon began penning MC Protocol 101 and President's Bible Chronicle II Betrayal in the Brotherhood.

In 2025 January, Black Dragon was again invited to be a featured speaker at the PROC.

In March of 2025 El Domino's song, "Diamond On My Heart" was remixed to feature Snoop Dogg rapping on the song. Black Dragon is now featured on a song with Snoop Dogg as a result.

In March of 2025 Black Dragon published *"Motorcycle Club Protocol 101"* his seventh book in the Motorcycle Club Bible series.

In December of 2025 Black Dragon published *"Robert's Rules of Order for Motorcycle Clubs"* the eighth book in The Motorcycle Club Bible series.

In January of 2026 Black Dragon published *"Art of War for Motorcycle Clubs"* with two cover selections, his ninth and tenth books in the Motorcycle Club Bible series.

In February of 2026 Black Dragon published "Motorcycle Club Chaplain's Handbook" his eleventh book in the Motorcycle Club Bible series.

Today Black Dragon is looking ahead to see where he can be of service to motorcycle clubs, riding clubs, social clubs, and biker organizations worldwide.

Black Dragon is formerly a senior lifer and East Coast Regional President in the Mighty Black Sabbath Motorcycle Club Nation.

Black Sabbath Forever Black Sabbath
A Breed Apart
Since 1974

www.blacksabbathmc.com

A NOTE FROM BLACK DRAGON

Now what? You have read the book, and you know the power of the information held within. I want you to know that you can help other bikers and clubs navigate their way through the murky waters of having a successful club life in their beloved MCs.

If you were helped, educated, or informed by this book there are a couple of simple things you can do to join me in remaking the MC world through knowledge, experience, education, and love:

1. If you believe "Motorcycle Club Chaplain's Handbook" has helped you then I ask that you spread the word by buying a copy for someone you think should have one.

2. Setup a reading group to discuss how this book applies to helping to better your MC. You can also write an honest review on social media, your blog, website, or on your favorite bookseller's website. There are countless ways you can help others by spreading this word. "Motorcycle Club Chaplain's Handbook" is not just a book worth reading, it is a vision and a plan worth following for every member to contribute positively to their MC. It is a vision worth sharing.

3. Enrich other MCs by buying this book for your brother MCs on the set with whom you share alliances. Imagine if brother MCs could have the benefit of the knowledge you have attained.

Thank you for your support! Send me an email anytime with questions, improvements, or your best MC tales!

blackdragon@blacksabbathmc.com

Buy The Art of War for Motorcycle Clubs

More from John E. "**Black Dragon**" Bunch II

Bunch Media Group LLC.

The Art of War for Motorcycle Clubs

Learn how to adapt the principles of Sun Tzu's ancient 13-chapter masterpiece about warfare directly to the modern traditional and outlaw motorcycle club world with no-BS, from the set to the set.

Buy Robert's Rules for Motorcycle Clubs

More from John E. "**Black Dragon**" Bunch II

Bunch Media Group LLC.

Robert's Rules for Motorcycle Clubs
Amazon #1 Best Seller

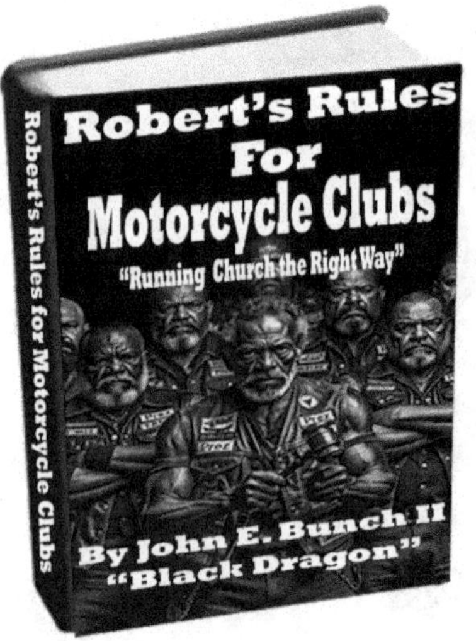

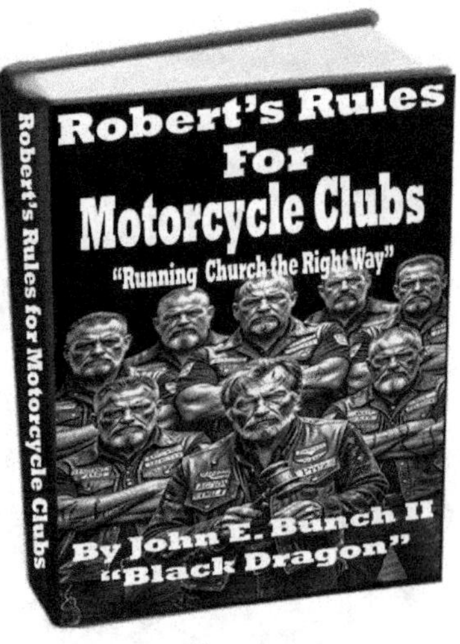

Learn how to run church the right way
For a traditional MC!
Order 24 hours per day (choose from 2 covers)
www.blackdragonsgear.com
Available from Kindle, Amazon.com, Audible, and retail bookstores.

Buy Prospect's Bible

More from John E. "**Black Dragon**" Bunch II

Bunch Media Group LLC.

Prospect's Bible
Amazon #1 Best Seller

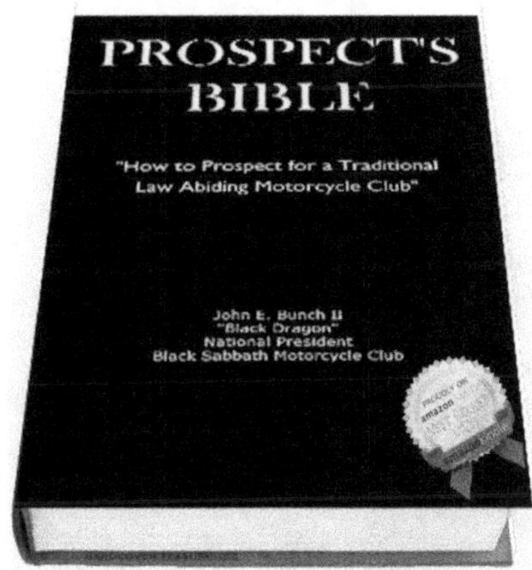

Learn how to prospect for
a traditional MC!
Order 24 hours per day
www.blackdragonsgear.com
Available from Kindle, Amazon.com, Audible, and retail bookstores.

Buy Sergeant-at-Arms Bible

More from John E. "**Black Dragon**" Bunch II

Bunch Media Group

Sergeant at Arms Bible
Amazon #1 Best Seller

Learn how to be the Sergeant-at-Arms for
a traditional MC!
Order 24 hours per day
www.blackdragonsgear.com
Available from Kindle, Amazon.com, Audible, and retail bookstores.

Buy Public Relations Officer's Bible

More from John E. "**Black Dragon**" Bunch II

Bunch Media Group

Motorcycle Clubs Public Relations Officer's Bible
Amazon #1 Best Seller

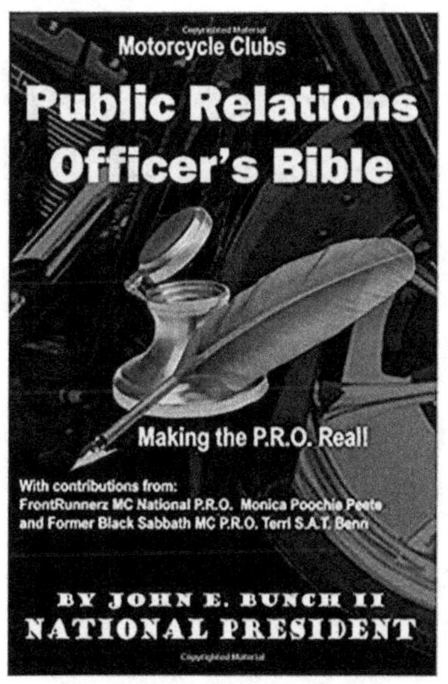

Learn how to be the Sergeant-at-Arms for
a traditional MC!
Order 24 hours per day
www.blackdragonsgear.com
Available from Kindle, Amazon.com, Audible, and retail bookstores.

Buy Social Club's Bible
Revival of the Women's Social Club Movement
'Lifting as We Climb"

More from John E. "**Black Dragon**" Bunch II
Bunch Media Group Amazon #1 Best Seller

Social Clubs Bible is a manual that teaches women who are interested in joining or are already part of Black women's social clubs. The book covers the history, rules, and protocols of the Black MC set. It also revisits the history of Black women's clubs and encourages today's social clubs to improve the African American MC set and communities.

Buy Prospect's Bible for Women's MCs
'How to Prospect for a Women's MC'

More from John E. "**Black Dragon**" Bunch II
Bunch Media Group Amazon #1 Best Seller

Learn how to define the MC Set, find a women's motorcycle club, and successfully prospect for it to win your status as a full patch sister in today's MC environment.

Buy Prospect's Motorcycle Club Protocol 101
'The Social Construct of Motorcycle Clubs'

More from John E. "**Black Dragon**" Bunch II
Bunch Media Group Amazon #1 Best Seller

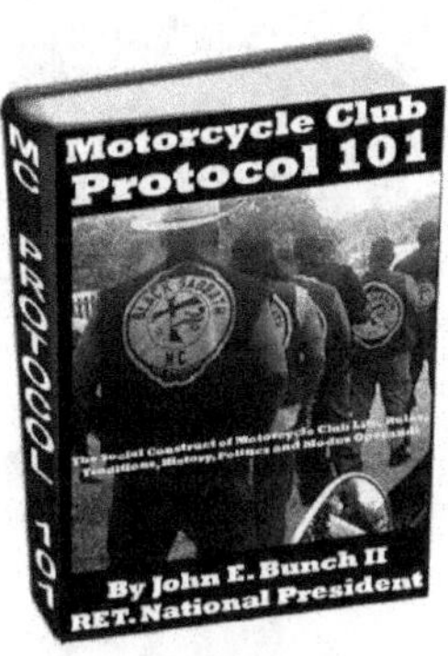

Instructs hang-arounds, prospects, and full patch members of motorcycle clubs the Social Construct of motorcycle club life, rules, traditions, history, and modus operandi."

BLACK SABBATH
National President

BlackDragonsGear.com

www.ingramcontent.com/pod-product-compliance
Lightning Source LLC
LaVergne TN
LVHW020718110826
845149LV00012B/2320

* 9 7 9 8 9 9 9 1 2 0 8 7 8 *